MACMILLAN
CONNECTIONS
READING PROGRAM

FRIENDS ALOFT

SENIOR AUTHORS

Virginia A. Arnold   Carl B. Smith

AUTHORS

James Flood   Diane Lapp

LITERATURE CONSULTANTS

Joan I. Glazer   Margaret H. Lippert

Macmillan/McGraw-Hill School Publishing Company
New York   Chicago   Columbus

ACKNOWLEDGMENTS

The publisher gratefully acknowledges permission to reprint the following copyrighted material:

"Alexander and the Wind-Up Mouse" is from ALEXANDER AND THE WIND-UP MOUSE by Leo Lionni. Copyright © 1969 by Leo Lionni. Reprinted by permission of Pantheon Books, a division of Random House, Inc. and by permission of Abelard-Schuman Ltd., London.

"Amelia's Flying Machine" is from AMELIA'S FLYING MACHINE by Barbara Shook Hazen. Copyright © 1977 by Barbara Shook Hazen. Reprinted by permission of the author.

"Berries" from LITTLE RACCOON AND POEMS FROM THE WOODS by Lilian Moore. Copyright © 1975 by Lilian Moore. Reprinted by permission of Marian Reiner for the author.

"The Big Balloon Race" is the adapted and abridged pages 23–62 from THE BIG BALLOON RACE by Eleanor Coerr. Text copyright © 1981 by Eleanor Coerr. Illustrations copyright © 1981 by Carolyn Croll. Reprinted by permission of Harper & Row, Publishers, Inc. and World's Work Ltd.

"Blueberries for Sal" is the text and specified illustrations from BLUEBERRIES FOR SAL by Robert McCloskey. Copyright 1948, renewed © 1976 by Robert McCloskey. Reprinted by permission of Viking-Penguin, Inc.

"Commander Toad and the Planet of the Grapes" from COMMANDER TOAD AND THE PLANET OF THE GRAPES by Jane Yolen. Text copyright © 1982 by Jane Yolen. Illustrations copyright © 1982 by Bruce Degen. Reprinted by permission of Coward, McCann & Geoghegan and Curtis Brown, Ltd.

"Earth, Moon, and Sun" from POEMS OF EARTH AND SPACE by Claudia Lewis. Text copyright © 1967 by Claudia Lewis. Reprinted by permission of the publisher, E. P. Dutton, a division of New American Library.

"The First Zeppelin" from I GO A-TRAVELING by James S. Tippett. Copyright 1929 by Harper & Row, Publishers, Inc. Renewed 1957 by James S. Tippett. Reprinted by permission of Harper and Row, Publishers, Inc.

"A Gift for Tía Rosa" is adapted from A GIFT FOR TÍA ROSA by Karen Taha, by permission of the publisher, Gemstone Books (Dillon Press, Inc.), 242 Portland Avenue South, Minneapolis, MN 55415.

"Harriet and William and the Terrible Creature" is an adaptation of HARRIET AND WILLIAM AND THE TERRIBLE CREATURE by Valerie Scho Carey, illustrations by Lynne Cherry. Text copyright © 1985 by Valerie Scho Carey. Illustrations copyright © 1985 by Lynne Cherry. Reprinted by permission of the publisher, E. P. Dutton, a division of New American Library.

Contents

5

6

8

Introducing Level 7
CARING

A friend in need is a friend indeed.

Friends who help you when you need them are friends who really care. In this unit, you will read about people who show they care about each other by working together and learning together. You will also learn that sometimes you can be your own best friend. How would you show someone that you really care?

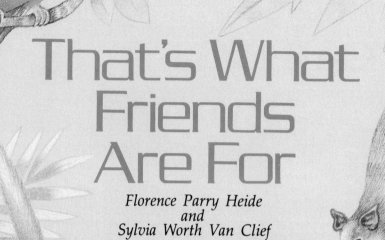

That's What Friends Are For

Florence Parry Heide
and
Sylvia Worth Van Clief

Everyone needs friends. You usually play
with your friends. You may work with them,
too. Can friends do other things for you?
Theodore thinks so. He asks his friends for
advice. To their surprise, not only Theodore but
also his friends get some good advice about
what friends are for.

Theodore, the elephant, is sitting in the middle of the forest. He has hurt his leg.

What a pity! Today Theodore was going to meet his cousin at the end of the forest.

"What can I do?" Theodore says. "My cousin is at the end of the forest, and here I am in the middle of the forest. And I have a bad leg, and I can't walk."

"I know what I'll do," Theodore says. "I'll ask my friends for advice. That's what friends are for."

11

Along comes Theodore's friend, the bird.

"Why are you sitting here in the middle of the forest?" asks the bird.

"Because I have a bad leg, and I can't walk. And I can't meet my cousin at the end of the forest," says Theodore.

"If *I* had a bad leg, I would fly to the end of the forest," says the bird to Theodore.

"It's nice of you to give advice," says Theodore to the bird.

"That's what friends are for," says the bird.

13

Along comes Theodore's friend, the monkey.

"Why are you sitting here in the middle of the forest?" asks the monkey.

"Because I have a bad leg, and I can't walk. And I can't fly. And I can't meet my cousin at the end of the forest," says Theodore.

"If *I* had a bad leg," says the monkey, "I would swing by my tail from the trees, like this."

"Well," says Theodore, "I may have a very weak *tail*, but I have a very strong *trunk*."

Theodore grabs a branch of the tree with his trunk . . .

Crash!

"Well, anyhow," says Theodore, "thank you for your advice."

"That's what friends are for," says the monkey.

15

Along comes Theodore's friend, the lion.

"Why are you sitting here in the middle of the forest?" asks the lion.

"Because I have a bad leg, and I can't walk. And I can't fly. And I can't swing from the trees by my tail (OR my trunk). And I can't meet my cousin at the end of the forest," says Theodore.

"If *I* had a bad leg," says the lion, "I would roar so loud that everyone in the whole forest would hear me, and come running to see what was the matter."

And he roars.

"What's all the noise?" the opossum asks. He is hanging upside down by his tail.

Theodore's friends all begin to talk at once. "Theodore can't fly," says the bird.

He can't get to the end of the forest to see his cousin," says the lion. "We are giving him advice. That's what friends are for."

"Nonsense," says the opossum. "Friends are to *help*. Bring the cousin to *Theodore*."

So all the friends go to find Theodore's cousin at the end of the forest.

And they bring the cousin to Theodore.

Theodore and the cousin and all the friends are having a party.

"Thank you for helping me," says Theodore to his friends.

"That's what friends are for," say the friends.

To give advice is very nice, but friends can do much more. Friends should always help a friend. That's what friends are for!

Thinking and Writing About the Selection

1. Whom did Theodore ask for advice?

2. Why couldn't Theodore walk to meet his cousin?

3. Why do you think the opossum gave Theodore good advice?

4. If you were Theodore's friend, what kind of advice would you have given him?

Applying the Key Skill
Cause of an Event

Number your paper from 1 to 3. Finish each sentence about the story "That's What Friends Are For." Write the sentence on your paper.

1. Theodore could not meet his cousin at the end of the forest because ___.

2. Theodore could not walk, so ___.

3. Theodore's friends gave him lots of advice because ___.

"Here come the elephants,

Here come the elephants, ten feet high,
elephants, elephants, heads in the sky.
Eleven great elephants intertwined,
one little elephant close behind.

Elephants over and elephants under
elephants bellow with elephant thunder.
Up on pedestals elephants hop,
elephants go and elephants stop.

20

ten feet high..."

Elephants quick and elephants slow,
elephants dancing to and fro.
Elephants, elephants twice times six,
elephants doing elephant tricks.

Elephants strutting, elephants strolling,
rollicking elephants frolicking, rolling.
Elephants forming an elephant arch,
elephants marching an elephant march.

Jack Prelutsky

Animals of Freedom

Gibbs Davis

Theodore and his friends knew each other well and liked to play and work together. Sometimes, even when you don't know someone well, you can still work together. A sculptor and some school children work together to make a special place in their neighborhood.

Many kinds of animals make their homes in a special place in New York City. This place is not a zoo. The animals are not real. They are sculptures made by school children of every age.

The set of animal sculptures is a gift. The gift is for all the children on this earth. You can go on a visit there. You may even touch the animals!

The person who brought this idea to life is the sculptor Greg Wyatt. He made a very large sculpture that stands in a park. The sculpture tells of Greg Wyatt's hope for peace. But Mr. Wyatt wanted to do something more.

He had a sculpture contest. Notices were sent to art teachers. Each sculpture could be a real or pretend animal. Each animal would stand for freedom. The entire sculpture could be no bigger than seven inches (almost 18 centimeters) tall and four inches (about 10 centimeters) wide. The children could make their animals out of clay, wood, or plaster.

More than 600 children made sculptures for the contest. Surely, Mr. Wyatt didn't think that many people would take part! There were 24 sculptures picked from the contest. They were placed in a ring around Mr. Wyatt's large sculpture.

Some of the children used clay to make their animals. To make a clay animal, begin with a ball of clay. The ball of clay should fit in your hand. Form one end until it looks like an egg. This can be the head. Now, pull out the other end of the clay ball to form the body. Pull out small bits of clay from the body. These bits can form the legs, the tail, and the ears of your animal.

Would you like your animal to have interesting skin? Use a pencil or stick to make lines in the skin. If you do something that you don't like, you can fix the animal. Rub a little water on the clay and try again.

There are already 24 different animal sculptures in the ring. The contest will go on every year until there are 120 animals in all. One girl made a sculpture of an elephant. She said she made it because "elephants don't fight with each other. They use their trunks to say 'hello' and 'good-bye.'" Another child made a tiger because "tigers are always nice to other animals."

There are also bears, owls, a bird, and a dog. You will see a fish, a lion, a monkey, and a turtle. Look for the two seals, a mother fox, and her baby. One day you may visit this special place in New York City. It is a good place to sit and think and rest. But don't be surprised when you say, "What a nice fox," and the person next to you says, "Thanks. I made it."

Thinking and Writing About the Selection

1. Who made the animal sculptures?

2. What is one way to make a clay animal?

3. Why do you think all the children wanted to make sculptures?

 4. What animal of freedom would you like to make out of clay?

Applying the Key Skill
Plural Nouns

Choose the word that correctly completes each sentence. Write the finished sentence.

1. Children made sculptures of ___ that stood for freedom. (animal, animals)

2. The entire sculpture could be no bigger than seven ___ tall. (inches, inch)

3. Many of the children used clay to form the ___ of their animals. (body, bodies)

4. One of the children made a sculpture of two ___. (foxes, fox)

SKILLS activity

BEST TITLE

A title tells the main idea of a story. It can describe the story in a few words, or it can give a hint about what will happen. The title should make you want to read the story.

ACTIVITY A Read the story about Mrs. Max's class. Think about a good title for the story. Then write the title you chose on your paper.

The children in Mrs. Max's class were sad. Their teacher was going away. They wanted to give her something to remember them by. Peter thought a painting of the class would be best. Meg said that each child could pick a friend to paint. The boys and girls put all their pictures on a big piece of paper. Mrs. Max loved her present.

The best title for this story is ____ .
a. A Sad Day
b. A Picture to Remember
c. Mrs. Max Paints the Class

ACTIVITY B Read the story about Buffy. Think about a good title for the story. Write the title on your paper.

Buffy is a different kind of dog. When my cat Tip had kittens, Buffy was very interested. She sniffed the kittens and licked them. Then Tip ran away. We couldn't find that cat anywhere. What would happen to the kittens? Buffy took care of that. She started to sleep in the cat bed with the kittens. She wouldn't let us touch them except to feed them. Does Buffy think she is a cat? Maybe she thinks the kittens are puppies. It doesn't matter because Buffy is such a good mother.

A good title for this story would be ____.

a. The Cat Who Ran Away
b. The Dog Who Thinks She Is a Cat
c. The Sad Kittens

The Bremen Town Musicians

Retold by Margaret H. Lippert

Friends can do many things together even when they run into bad times. The animal friends in this story help each other to be musicians.

The Players

Donkey	**Head Robber**
Dog	**Big Robber**
Cat	**Little Robber**
Rooster	**Storyteller**

ACT ONE

Storyteller: There was once a farmer who had a donkey. The donkey had worked hard for many years, but now he was getting too old to work. One day the farmer was talking to a friend about selling his donkey, and the donkey heard him.

Donkey: I can't believe that after all my hard work, the farmer has decided to sell me. No one will want to buy an old donkey like me. I will run away to Bremen town and be a musician there.

Storyteller: So in the morning the donkey set off down the road to Bremen. Soon he came to a dog lying in the road.

Donkey: Why are you lying there in the road?

Dog: I need to rest. I have just run a long way and I'm tired.

Donkey: Where are you going?

Dog: I don't know. I am running away because my master is angry with me. I am getting old and can't run as fast as I once could. Last night when I let a fox run off with a nice, fat chicken, my master told his daughter to kiss me good-bye. He said that I am no longer worth the food I eat, so I decided to run away.

Donkey: Why don't you come with me? I am going to Bremen to be a musician. You, too, have a beautiful voice. We can make music together.

Storyteller: So the dog went along with the donkey. Soon they came to a cat who was looking very sad.

Donkey: Why are you so sad?

Cat: I am about to die. Last night I heard the miller talking to his family. He said he doesn't want me anymore because I am getting too old to catch mice. My teeth are not as sharp as they once were, so the mice get away. The miller said he is going to toss me into the lake tomorrow, and I can't swim.

Donkey: Don't be sad any longer. Come along with us. We are off to Bremen town to be musicians. With your beautiful voice, you can help us earn money for food.

Storyteller: So the cat followed the donkey and the dog down the road. Before long they saw a rooster crowing.

Donkey: I never heard a rooster crowing so late in the morning. What is the matter?

Rooster: Soon I will leave the earth, and this is my last song. I just heard the farmer tell his wife that I am getting old and sleep too late to wake them up in the morning. He told her to make me into soup for dinner.

Donkey: Why then you must come with us! We are going to Bremen to be musicians. With your crowing we will be the envy of all the other musicians there.

Storyteller: So the rooster went down the road with the donkey, the dog, and the cat.

ACT TWO

Storyteller: The friends walked on and on, but they could not get to Bremen that day. When it began to get dark, they decided to look for a place to spend the night. Way back in the woods they saw a little light. They agreed to go toward it, hoping to find something to eat. They walked into the dark woods, and after a long time they saw a house through the trees.

Donkey: There must be someone at home. You hide behind this clump of bushes, while I go and look through the window.

Storyteller: The donkey went alone to the house and peeked through the window. There he saw a band of robbers eating dinner. On the table was lots of gold, and on shelves behind the robbers were stored all kinds of food.

Donkey: This is the place for us. Now all we have to do is scare the robbers away.

Storyteller: The donkey went back to the other animals behind the bushes, and together they made a plan. First the donkey went over to the window. Then the dog got on the donkey's back, the cat got on the dog's back, and the rooster flew up on top of the cat's back. Then they all began to sing. Suddenly all four animals fell through the window. The robbers were so scared by all that noise that they ran out of the house into the woods.

Donkey: We did it! We scared them away!

Dog: Look at all this good food. Come on, I'm ready to eat.

Storyteller: They all sat down at the table and ate until they were full.

Cat: My, but I'm tired. The fireplace is still warm. I think I'll sleep there.

Dog: I think I'll sleep here behind the door.

Donkey: I'll go outside and sleep in front of the house.

Rooster: I think I'll make it up to the roof. Good night!

Storyteller: Soon all the animals were asleep. As the robbers began to think about their dinner and about their gold, they decided they had made a mistake and had been scared away too quickly. They went back toward their house and saw that it was dark and quiet.

Head Robber: It looks as though our house is empty now. Let's go back in.

Big Robber: Not so fast, Boss. One of us should go in first to be sure all of them are gone. How about it, Shorty?

Little Robber: Don't look at me, Slim. I always do all the dirty work.

Head Robber: He's right. You go ahead, Slim. Look all around. If everything seems fine, whistle. When we hear you whistle, we'll come in. Good luck, and be careful.

Little Robber: Don't forget to open the front door slowly so it doesn't squeak.

Storyteller: The head robber and the little robber waited behind a clump of trees while the big robber went into the house. They were listening for a whistle, but the big robber never whistled. He was careful, but when he opened the front door it did squeak a little. The cat opened her eyes. The robber saw the cat's eyes gleam in the fireplace. He blew on them to give himself more light, but instead he got the surprise of his life. The cat jumped up and scratched him in the face with her claws. As the robber backed out of the door, the dog bit him on the leg. Then the donkey kicked him as he ran outside.

Big Robber: Help! Help! I'm going to die.

Rooster: *(from the roof)* COCK-A-DOODLE-DOO!

39

Storyteller: The big robber ran away and banged right into the other robbers, who were still standing behind the trees.

Head Robber: What happened? You look awful.

Big Robber: I FEEL awful. My leg is bleeding and I'm hurting all over. I envy you, Shorty. You have all the luck.

Little Robber: Well don't be shy. Tell us what happened.

Big Robber: There's a band of strong people in there. One in the fireplace scratched me in the face. Another one behind the door cut me in the leg. A third one outside hit me with a huge stick. Another one on the roof called out, "CATCH THAT MAN NOW, DO!"

Head Robber: Let's go. We'll never come back.

Storyteller: The robbers ran into the woods and never did go back. But the animals had found what they wanted, a warm, dry house to sleep in, and enough food stored up to last them a long time. They may live there still, making beautiful music together under the stars.

Thinking and Writing About the Selection

1. What did the animals see through the trees in the dark woods?

2. Why were the animals going to Bremen town?

3. How do you think the animals were like musicians when they scared the robbers?

4. If you were one of the animals, how would you have scared the robbers away?

Applying the Key Skill
Final Consonant Clusters

Use the letters *nd, nt, mp,* and *lt* to finish the words. Write the words on your paper.

Cat, Dog, Rooster, and Donkey we___ to Bremen. They fe___ that they wanted to play music. They could not wait to sing again. The ba___ saw lots of people. As the animals started to sing, the people began to ju___ up and down.

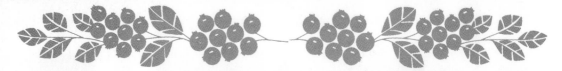

BLUEBERRIES

FOR SAL

Robert McCloskey

The Bremen town musicians fooled the robbers with a sound. Have you ever been fooled by a sound? Sometimes you may think you know what a sound is, but it turns out to be something else. In this story, Little Sal goes blueberry picking with her mother. Read to see what happens when she gets lost in the woods and begins to follow a sound that she *thinks* is her mother!

42

One day, Little Sal went with her
mother to Blueberry Hill to pick blueberries.

Little Sal brought along her small tin
pail and her mother brought her large
tin pail to put berries in. "We will take
our berries home and can them," said her
mother. "Then we will have food for
the winter."

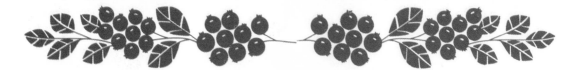

Little Sal picked three berries and
dropped them in her tin pail . . . *kuplink,
kuplank, kuplunk!*

She picked three more berries and ate
them. Then she picked more berries and
dropped one in the pail—*kuplunk!* And the
rest she ate. Then Little Sal ate all four
blueberries out of her pail.

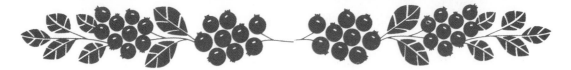

Her mother walked slowly through the bushes, picking blueberries as she went and putting them in her pail. Little Sal struggled along behind, picking blueberries and eating every single one.

Little Sal hurried ahead and dropped a blueberry in her mother's pail. It didn't sound *kuplink!* because the bottom of the pail was already covered with berries. She reached down inside to get her berry back. Though she really didn't mean to, she pulled out a large handful, because there were so many blueberries right up close to the one she had put in.

Her mother stopped picking and said, "Now, Sal, you run along and pick your own berries. Mother wants to take her berries home and can them for next winter."

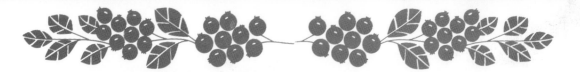

Her mother went back to her picking, but Little Sal, because her feet were tired of standing and walking, sat down in the middle of a large clump of bushes and ate blueberries.

On the other side of Blueberry Hill, Little Bear came with his mother to eat blueberries.

"Little Bear," she said, "eat lots of berries and grow big and fat. We must store up food for the long, cold winter."

Little Bear followed behind his mother
as she walked slowly through the bushes
eating berries. Little Bear stopped now and
then to eat berries.

Then he had to hustle along to catch up!

Because his feet were tired of hustling, he
picked out a large clump of bushes and sat
down right in the middle and ate blueberries.

Over on the other side of the hill, Little
Sal ate all of the berries she could reach from
where she was sitting, then she started out
to find her mother.

She heard a noise from
around a rock and thought,
"That is my mother walking
along!"

But it was a mother crow and her
children, and they stopped eating berries
and flew away, saying, "Caw, Caw, Caw."
Then she heard another noise in the bushes
and thought, "That is *surely* my mother
and I will go that way."

But it was Little Bear's mother instead.
She was tramping along, eating berries,
and thinking about storing up food for
the winter. Little Sal tramped right
along behind.

By this time, Little Bear had eaten all the berries he could reach without moving from his clump of bushes. Then he hustled off to catch up with his mother. He hunted and hunted but his mother was nowhere to be seen. He heard a noise from over a stump and thought, "That is my mother walking along."

But it was a mother partridge and her children. They stopped eating berries and hurried away. Then he heard a noise in the bushes and thought, "That is surely *my* mother. I will hustle that way!"

But it was Little Sal's mother instead! She was walking along, picking berries, and thinking about canning them for next winter. Little Bear hustled right along behind.

Little Bear and Little Sal's mother and Little Sal and Little Bear's mother were all mixed up with each other among the blueberries on Blueberry Hill.

49

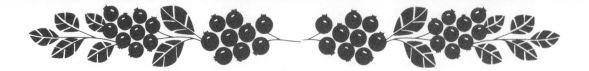

Little Bear's mother heard Sal walking
along behind and thought it was Little
Bear and she said, "Little Bear," *munch,
munch,* "Eat all you—" *gulp,* "can possibly
hold!" *swallow.* Little Sal said nothing. She
picked three berries and dropped them,
kuplink, kuplank, kuplunk, in her small
tin pail.

Little Bear's mother turned around
to see what on earth could make a noise
like *kuplunk!*

"Garumpf!" she cried, choking on a
mouthful of berries, "This is not my child!
Where is Little Bear?" She took one good
look and backed away. (She was old
enough to be shy of people, even a very
small person like Little Sal.) Then she
turned around and walked off very fast to
hunt for Little Bear.

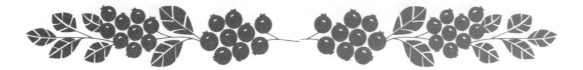

Little Sal's mother heard Little Bear tramping along behind and thought it was Little Sal. She kept right on picking and thinking about canning blueberries for next winter.

Little Bear padded up and peeked into her pail. Of course, he only wanted to taste a *few* of what was inside, but there were so many and they were so close together, that he tasted a Tremendous Mouthful by mistake. "Now, Sal," said Little Sal's mother without turning around, "you run along and pick your own berries. Mother wants to can these for next winter." Little Bear tasted another Tremendous Mouthful, and almost spilled the entire pail of blueberries!

Little Sal's mother turned around and gasped, "My Goodness, *you* are not Little Sal! Where, oh where, is my child?"

Little Bear just sat munching and munching and swallowing and licking his lips.

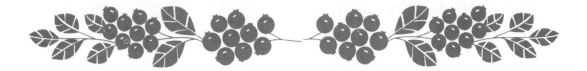

Little Sal's mother slowly backed away.
(She was old enough to be shy of bears,
even very small bears like Little Bear.)
Then she turned and walked away quickly
to look for Little Sal.

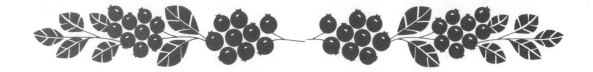

She hadn't gone very far before she heard a *kuplink! kuplank! kuplunk!*

She knew just what made that kind of a noise!

Little Bear's mother had not hunted very long before she heard a hustling sound that stopped now and then to munch and swallow. She knew just what made that kind of a noise.

Little Bear and his mother went home down one side of Blueberry Hill, eating blueberries all the way, and full of food stored up for next winter.

And Little Sal and her mother went down the other side of Blueberry Hill, picking berries all the way, and drove home with food to can for next winter—
a whole pail of blueberries and
three more besides.

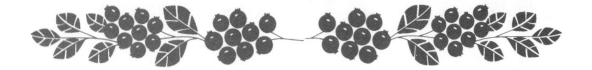

Thinking and Writing About the Selection

1. What did Little Sal do when her feet were tired?

2. Why did Little Sal and her mother go to pick blueberries?

3. Why didn't Little Sal's mother notice right away that Little Sal was not with her?

4. How have you ever been fooled by a sound?

Applying the Key Skill
Grid Maps

Use the map to answer the questions.

1. Where is Little Sal's house?

2. Where is Little Bear?

3. Where is Little Sal?

Key:

	Little Sal's house
	tree stumps
	blueberry bushes
	Little Bear
	Little Sal

	A	B	C	D
1	🏠			
2		🐻		
3		🌿		👧

55

Berries

Hurry

Berry

Hurry!

Fatten in the sun.

Huckleberry

Gooseberry

Dribble—dribble juice berry

Raspberry

Hackberry

Nibble—nibble blackberry

Hurry

Everyone!

The way

Berries

Grow

Is

TOO

SLOW.

Lilian Moore

57

A Gift For Tía Rosa

Karen Taha

Learning something new with a good friend can be fun. Carmela's friend Tía Rosa has taught her how to knit. Tía Rosa helps Carmela with a scarf she is knitting for her father. But Tía Rosa gets very sick and must stay in bed. Carmela looks for a way to show her friend she will always remember her.

"Around, over, through, and pull. Around, over, through, and pull," Carmela said as she worked at her knitting.

"I'll get it!" Carmela shouted, and she jumped up. "Tía Rosa!" she said with a smile when she heard the voice on the telephone. "You must see Papá's scarf. It's almost finished . . . Yes, I'll be right there!"

Carmela ran to see her mother. "Mamá! Tía Rosa wants to see the scarf." Carmela's mother just smiled and shook her head. Carmela put her knitting into her school bag. "I'm going to make Tía Rosa a surprise when Papá's scarf is finished!" she called as she ran out.

She ran across the yard to Tía Rosa's front porch, and there was Tío Juan at the door. He looked the same as ever, except that his eyes looked sad. "*Hola*, Carmelita," he said, and he bent to kiss her. He led her to Tía Rosa's bedroom. "Tía Rosa is sitting up in bed. She's tired, but she wanted to see her Carmelita."

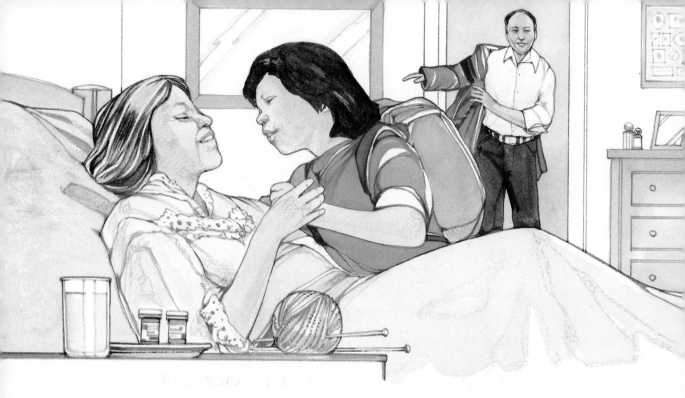

Tía Rosa in bed! In all her eight years
Carmela had never seen Tía Rosa sick.
Tío Juan held her hand as she peeked into
the bedroom.

"Carmelita, come give me a hug!" said Tía
Rosa with a big smile. "I've missed you! Let's
look at what you have been knitting." Carmela
handed her the scarf. Tía Rosa smiled. "I
knew you'd be good at knitting! Your papá
will be so happy!" she said. "Tomorrow we'll
work together. You'll learn how to tie the end
so it looks really beautiful, and I will start on
the pink baby blanket for my granddaughter!"

Carmela laughed. "How do you know that the baby will be a girl?" she asked.

"Because," answered Tía Rosa with a smile, "anyone who has six children, all boys, should have a granddaughter!"

Carmela came back the next day, and the next, and every day for a whole week. Tía Rosa stayed in her room, and Tío Juan put a chair by the bed for Carmela. Together the two friends worked on their knitting. Sometimes they hardly said a word, and other times they would spend the afternoon telling stories and giggling together.

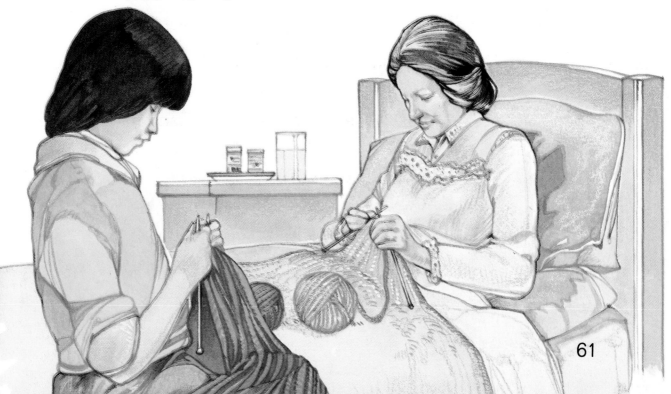

"Why does Tía Rosa stay in bed all the time?" Carmela asked her father at breakfast one day.

Her father looked away, and then he took Carmela's hands in his. "Tía Rosa is very sick, Carmela. I don't think she can get well," he said.

"But Papá," said Carmela. "I have been sick a lot. Remember when Tía Rosa stayed with me when you and Mamá had to go away?"

"Yes," answered her father. "But Tía Rosa . . ."

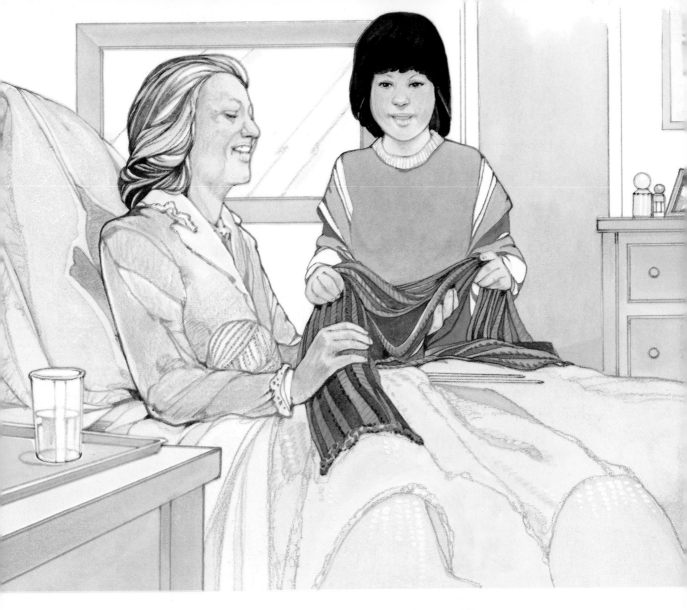

Carmela didn't listen. "Now I will stay
with Tía Rosa until she gets well, too," she said.

Every afternoon Carmela worked on her
father's scarf. With Tía Rosa's help she would
be able to have the scarf finished long before
his birthday.

One Saturday morning when Carmela
went to see Tía Rosa, Tío Juan didn't come to
the door. "That's funny," she thought. She
hurried home to find her mother. "Tía Rosa
isn't home," said Carmela sadly.

When she saw her father's sad face,
Carmela felt cold. He gave Carmela and her
mother a hug and whispered, "Tía Rosa is
gone. She died early this morning."

No, her father's words couldn't be true.
Carmela didn't believe it. Tía Rosa gone? She
had just seen her yesterday. Tía Rosa would
come back. She had always come back before.

"It's not true!" cried Carmela. She ran out of the room, out the front door, and through the yard to Tía Rosa's house. She banged on the door until her hands hurt. At last she sat down on the steps.

Later her father came. She cried in his lap until she wasn't able to cry anymore. At last they walked slowly home.

The next days were long and lonely for Carmela. She didn't want to look at Papá's beautiful finished scarf. She didn't want to feel the knitting needles in her hands ever again.

One day Carmela said to her mother, "Tía Rosa died before I could give her anything, Mamá. I was going to surprise her. Now it's too late."

"Carmela, Tía Rosa didn't mean for her kindness to be given back to her. She wanted it to be passed on," said her mother. "That way a bit of Tía Rosa will never die."

"But I wanted to give something to her!" shouted Carmela. "Just to Tía Rosa. To show her that I loved her!"

"She knew that, Carmela. Every smile and hug and visit told her that you loved her," said her mother. "Now it's Tío Juan who needs our love. He will be very lonely."

The next night Carmela's mother asked Tío Juan to dinner. Carmela met him at the door and gave him a big hug.

For the first time in a week, Tío Juan smiled. "Carmelita, tomorrow you must come next door. I would like you to meet my new granddaughter. She was born yesterday. Her parents have named her Rosita, little Rose, after her grandmother."

Carmelita looked down so Tío Juan would
not see how her eyes had filled. Tía Rosa
knew the baby would be a girl. Then Carmela
remembered the blanket that Tía Rosa had not
finished. "Now I know what I can give!"
she said.

Carmela came back with Tía Rosa's big
knitting bag. Slowly she pulled out the little
pink blanket and began knitting.

"Around, over, through, and pull.
Around, over, through, and pull." Carmela
smiled. At last she had a gift for Tía Rosa.

Thinking and Writing About the Selection

1. What did Carmela want to do after Papá's scarf was finished?

2. Why did Tía Rosa start knitting a pink baby blanket?

3. Why do you think Carmela wanted to show Tía Rosa the scarf she was knitting?

 4. Would you act in the same way Carmela did? Why or why not?

Applying the Key Skill
Contractions

Number your paper from 1 to 8. Write the words below:

1. I will   2. I am

3. she is   4. you would

5. was not   6. that is

7. did not   8. it is

Then look back at "A Gift for Tía Rosa." Find and write the contractions that stand for each set of words.

SKILLS activity

HOMOPHONES

Some words sound the same but have different meanings. They have different spellings, too. You need to read the whole sentence to know which meaning of the word to use. Word pairs like this are called **homophones**.

> The children walked near the <u>sea</u>.
> They wanted to <u>see</u> a whale.

The words <u>sea</u> and <u>see</u> sound alike, but they have different spellings and meanings. <u>Sea</u> and <u>see</u> are homophones.

Read each word in the box. Then read each sentence. Choose the word that makes the sentence correct. Write the whole sentence on your paper.

bear	bare

1. The ___ stood up on two legs.
2. Don't walk with ___ feet.

70

| week | weak |

3. Next ____ we are going away.

4. The old dog was sick and very ____ .

| rode | road |

5. The train tracks crossed the ____ .

6. We ____ in the back of the truck.

| write | right |

7. You should turn ____ at the light.

8. Please ____ your name on the list.

| peace | piece |

9. We need ____ and quiet today.

10. This ____ of cake is too big for me to eat.

MY FRIEND JACOB

Lucille Clifton

illustrated by Thomas DiGrazia

Friends learn together. They can teach each other, too. Tía Rosa taught Carmela how to knit. Sam and Jacob are good friends who teach each other new things. Jacob learns something special from Sam and gives his friend a surprise.

My best friend lives next door. His name is Jacob. He is my very very best friend.

We do things together, Jacob and me. We love to play basketball together. Jacob always makes a basket on the first try.

He helps me to learn how to hold the ball so that I can make baskets, too.

My mother used to say "Be careful with Jacob and that ball; he might hurt you." But now she doesn't. She knows that Jacob wouldn't hurt anybody, especially his very very best friend.

I love to sit on the steps and watch the cars
go by with Jacob. He knows the name of every
kind of car. Even if he only sees it just for a
minute, Jacob can tell you the kind of car.

He is helping me be able to tell the cars, too. When I make a mistake, Jacob never ever laughs. He just says, "No no, Sam, try again."

And I do. He is my best best friend.

When I have to go to the store, Jacob goes with me to help me. His mother used to say "You don't have to have Jacob tagging along with you like that, Sammy." But now she doesn't. She knows we like to go to the store together. Jacob helps me to carry, and I help Jacob to remember.

"Red is for stop," I say if Jacob forgets. "Green is for go."

"Thank you, Sam," Jacob always says.

Jacob's birthday and my birthday are two days apart. Sometimes we celebrate together.

Last year he made me a surprise. He had been having a secret for weeks and weeks, and my mother knew, and his mother knew, but they wouldn't tell me.

Jacob would stay in the house in the afternoon for half an hour every day and not say anything to me when he came out. He would just smile and smile.

On my birthday, my mother made a cake for me with eight candles, and Jacob's mother made a cake for him with seventeen candles. We sat on the porch and sang and blew out our candles. Jacob blew out all of his in one breath because he's bigger.

Then my mother smiled and Jacob's mother smiled and said, "Give it to him, Jacob dear." My friend Jacob smiled and handed me a card.

HAPPY BIRTHDAY SAM
JACOB

He had printed it all himself! All by himself, my name and everything! It was neat!

My very best friend Jacob does so much helping me, I wanted to help him, too. One day I decided to teach him how to knock.

Jacob will just walk into somebody's house if he knows them. If he doesn't know them, he will stand by the door until somebody notices him and lets him in.

"I wish Jacob would knock on the door," I heard my mother say.

So I decided to help him learn. Every day I would tell Jacob, but he would always forget. He would just open the door and walk right in.

My mother said probably it was too hard for him and I shouldn't worry about it. But I felt bad because Jacob always helped me so much, and I wanted to be able to help him, too.

I kept telling him and he kept forgetting, so one day I just said, "Never mind, Jacob, maybe it is too hard."

"What's the matter, Sam?" Jacob asked me.

"Never mind, Jacob" was all I said.

Next day, at dinnertime, we were sitting in our dining room when me and my mother and my father heard this real loud knocking at the door. Then the door popped open and Jacob stuck his head in.

"I'm knocking, Sam!" he yelled.

Boy, I jumped right up from the table and went grinning and hugged Jacob, and he grinned and hugged me, too. He is my very very very best friend in the whole world!

Thinking and Writing About the Selection

1. What do Sam and Jacob like to do together?

2. How does Jacob surprise Sam on his birthday?

3. Why do you think Sam told Jacob that maybe learning to knock was too hard?

4. How could you teach a friend something?

Applying the Key Skill
Best Title

Look back at "My Friend Jacob." Write a sentence that tells why this was a good title for the story. Now look at these titles for the same story. Which one do you like best and why?

a. Learning From Each Other

b. Sam and Jacob Go Shopping

c. I Teach Jacob to Knock

Lucille Clifton

Children and family are very important in Lucille Clifton's life and work. She was one of four children growing up near Buffalo, New York. "We didn't have much money," Clifton recalls, "but we had a lot of love." Now she is a successful writer with over twenty books of fiction and poetry for children and adults. And she has six children of her own.

"I write in spurts," says Clifton. "I never do all the things I'm supposed to do, like write at a set time. And I can't write if it's quiet." Clifton may break many of the rules of writing, but in books like *My Friend Jacob* she has given us people to remember.

More to Read   *All Us Come Cross the Water, Three Wishes, Everett Anderson's Nine Month Long*

PLEASE FOLLOW DIRECTIONS!

One way to teach people to follow directions is to show them, either by actions or by pictures. It also helps to *tell* them exactly what to do. Give directions in small steps and in the correct order. Use the words *first, second,* and *next* in your directions.

Look at the directions below for making a toy airplane. Write the directions in the right order on your paper. Use the words *first, second, next,* and *last* to help you.

Next, glue small wings to the tail.
Last, glue wheels at dots under each wing, and under the front of the plane.
First, glue the body of the plane together.
Second, glue large wings to Part A.

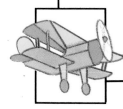

SKATING *for a* GOLD MEDAL

Lisa Yount

Sam and Jacob helped each other learn new things because they were good friends. Sometimes, though, you can help yourself by being your own best friend. Olympic ice skater Tiffany Chin gets help from her family and coach. But when she skates she knows she has to count on herself. Read to see why Tiffany thinks that "If you believe you can do something, you usually can."

Tiffany Chin's love of skating began with a pair of ice skates that cost one dollar. Tiffany Chin's mother saw them at a neighborhood sale. She thought Tiffany might like them. So she brought them home.

Tiffany was eight years old then. She did like the skates. But when she tried to skate in them, she got a surprise. She fell down! She and her mother looked hard at the skates. They were toy skates.

That did not stop Tiffany though. She had decided she liked skating. Her parents soon bought her some real skates.

Can Tiffany Chin be one of the best figure skaters in America? Just about everyone who knows skating thinks she may be. Many think she will soon be the best in the world.

Tiffany thinks she can be the best, too. But she knows that plenty of practice and hard work lie ahead. She has to skate for a long time each day. She has to go to school, too. She does not have much time to see friends.

Tiffany's family keeps her from being lonely. They help her in other ways, too. Tiffany's mother takes Tiffany back and forth to her skating coach. This means a long car trip three days a week. Tiffany is learning from her father not to be scared when everyone watches her skate. Even Tiffany's grandma and grandpa have helped her. They came from the island country of Taiwan. They have taught Tiffany wise ideas from China.

Tiffany's coach gives Tiffany plenty of help, too. He helps her make her body stronger. He also shows her how to make her skating seem easy. Her coach makes Tiffany practice the strokes of each figure over and over.

Even with all the help she gets, only Tiffany can make herself a world skating star. Some skating stars want to win more than anything else. Tiffany is not one of them. "I have to put on that feeling like a coat," she says. "When I skate, I forget about the world. I don't worry about what my mother or my coach thinks. I just skate my best."

Tiffany has learned to think in a way that helps her win. "If you believe you can do something, you usually can," she says. Once Tiffany was in a two-day contest. On the first day she did not skate well. Her strokes were not quite right. She tried to make a jump. Instead, she lost her balance and fell. Everyone had been sure she would win.

Tiffany was stubborn and would not give up. "I have to count more on myself," she said. "How can I skate better tomorrow?"

The next day, Tiffany began her skating with three jumps. They were as hard as the one that had made her fall. She did not fall this time. She went on to win the contest.

At the Winter Olympic Games, there is an even bigger skating contest. The games are held every four years. The skating stars of the world try to win this contest. The one who does gets a gold medal. Tiffany Chin is hoping to win that medal in 1988.

Tiffany has already been in the Olympic Games. She was part of the United States skating team in 1984. She was the first person on the team to have a family from a country in Asia. At that time, three people skated better than Tiffany. Next time she does not plan to let anyone do better.

Whirling and sliding back and forth across the ice, Tiffany seems to be flying. She seems to be part of the music. When people watch Tiffany, they do not think about how hard she has worked. They do not think about her strong ankles or good balance. They do not think about the help her family and her coach give Tiffany. They only think how beautiful her skating is. Tiffany does more than just skate well. She makes magic.

Thinking and Writing About the Selection

1. What does Tiffany have to do each day?

2. How does Tiffany's family help her?

3. How do you think Tiffany makes magic?

 4. If you could be a star of any sport, which would you pick? Why?

Applying the Key Skill
Homophones

Read each sentence. Find the word that correctly completes the sentence. Then write that word on your paper.

1. Tiffany does not have much time to ___ her friends, because she must practice her skating.

   a. see   b. sea

2. Tiffany practices for many ___ each day.

   a. ours   b. hours

3. On the first day of the contest, Tiffany's strokes were not quite ___.

   a. right   b. write

Kate can Skate

by Helen D. Olds

Tiffany Chin didn't let her first fall stop her from going on to be a top skater. In this story, Kate gets a pair of roller skates for the first time. Will Kate let her first fall keep her from learning how to skate?

Kate was seven years old, but she did not know how to roller skate. That was because she lived in the country, and there were no sidewalks.

One spring day, Mother said, "Kate, Daddy and I have to go on a trip. We can't take you. You will visit Grandma for three days."

Kate loved Grandma, but she was not sure about staying with her for three days. Grandma lived in the city.

She asked her mother, "Will I have fun? Where will I play?"

Mother laughed. "There are parks, playgrounds, and sidewalks to roller skate on."

"But I don't know how to roller skate," said Kate.

"You'll learn," Mother said. "I'll buy you a pair of skates."

When Mother said goodby to Kate at Grandma's house, she gave her the new skates.

Kate sat on the porch after Mother had gone. Just then two girls came out of the house next door. They were on skates. "I'm Beth," said one of the girls.

"I'm Jo," said the other. "Come and skate with us."

Kate shook her head. "I don't know how."

The girls looked surprised. "Kate— can't—skate!" they said and on they went down the sidewalk. Their words rang like a song, *Kate Can't Skate, Kate Can't Skate.*

Kate put on her skates. She held on to the porch and stood up. My, but she felt tall. She tried to walk on the skates. She took one step, then another. She stood still, wobbling on the skates.

Kate began rolling, rolling on the skates. Oh, she was going to fall! She tried not to, but her ankle turned. Down she went on the sidewalk.

GUY CLAVERIE

Kate was not hurt much, just a scratch on her knee. She must have looked funny, for the two girls came skating back, giggling.

Jo said, "I'll get a bandage."

Beth said, "I fell too when I was learning. Everyone does. You'll learn."

But Kate was cross. "No!" she shouted, brushing Jo aside. She took off the skates and ran into the house.

The next morning Kate felt very lonely as she sat on the steps. Everything was quiet except for the creak of the clothes dryer in the backyard. It was a whirling clothes dryer that went around like a merry-go-round. The backyard was very small and every inch of it was cement.

Kate was wishing for someone to play with, something to do. Could she learn to skate and surprise the girls?

I'll try, she decided.

If only she had someone to hold her up, she could learn to skate, she was sure.

As Kate dug into the hall closet for her skates, Grandpa's umbrella with the big handle fell off the hook. Kate thought maybe she could lean on it.

She went to the backyard to practice. The dryer was going round and round. Kate had another idea.

She put on her skates, and then she stood up. She hooked the handle of the umbrella over the clothes dryer. She held on to the umbrella and took a step, a sliding stroke, the way she had seen the sisters skate.

The clothes dryer moved, and so did Kate! The wind pushed her. Round and round went the dryer. Round and round went Kate, hanging on to the umbrella. The skates did not seem to go as fast as they had yesterday. Kate was glad about that. She was skating! It was fun.

GUY CLAVERIE

100

After a while she let go of the umbrella and tried skating alone. She went a few strokes, then fell over, but she wasn't hurt. Would she ever learn?

Kate got up and held on to the umbrella again. She was learning to lift her feet, how to make them slide, how to balance her body. Leaning forward a little helped, she found.

Soon she tried skating between the houses. Stroke, slide, left foot, right foot. She was really skating now! Back and forth she went across the cement driveway, from one house to the other. She fell a few times but that did not bother her.

Soon she saw Jo and Beth coming down the street. Kate skated down the sidewalk to meet them. Her ankles began to wobble but she did not fall.

"Why, Kate! You can *skate!*" they said. "We'll get our skates, too."

When the girls came back, they all joined hands, with Kate in the middle. Away they went down the sidewalk. It was like magic! Like flying, Kate thought.

"Tomorrow's Saturday," said Jo. "We can skate all day."

Beth said, "I'm glad Kate can skate."

Thinking and Writing About the Selection

1. What kind of clothes dryer was in the backyard?

2. How did Kate learn to skate?

3. Why do you think Kate was cross after she fell?

 4. Have you ever tried to learn something on your own? What happened?

Applying the Key Skill
Multiple-Meaning Words

Find the meaning of each underlined word. Write the word on your paper.

1. The girls saw Kate <u>land</u> on the sidewalk when she tried to skate.

   a. earth   b. come down   c. country

2. Kate decided to take a <u>rest</u> before trying to skate again.

   a. sleep or nap

   b. the last part of something

   c. play

SKATING SONG

Never stopping
Once you've gone,
Never looking
At the lawn,
Whizzing down
From crack to crack,
April whistling
At your back.
Spinning wheels
On bumpy ground,
Sidewalks sing
A hollow sound.

Over stones and twigs and holes,
Over mud and sticks and poles,
Past the house,
Past the trees,
Swinging arms and bending knees,
Past the fence posts,
Past the gates,
Here we come
On roller skates.

Myra Cohn Livingston

WRITING activity

FRIENDLY LETTER

Prewrite

Learning new things can be fun, but not always easy. Read "Kate Can Skate" again. Find the things that happened to Kate as she was learning to skate.

Of course half the fun of learning something is telling a friend about it. You are going to write a letter to a friend about something you have learned. Maybe you can tell about learning to swim, skate, or how to play a new game. You might tell the steps you follow to write a story or paint a picture.

Before you write, you need to think about a plan. Use these ideas in your plan:

1. Make a list of the things that happened to you as you were learning.
2. In what order did the things happen? Use words like *first*, *next*, and *last* to show the order.
3. What information do you need for the heading, greeting, and closing of your letter?

Write

1. Write your heading and greeting.
2. Now look at your plan. The first sentence in the body of your letter should tell what you learned. Then write other sentences about what happened as you were learning.
3. Try to use Vocabulary Treasures in your letter.
4. Write the closing of your letter.

Vocabulary Treasures	
able	funny
careful	practice

Revise

Read your letter. Have a friend read it, too. Think about these ideas as you revise.

1. Did the body of your letter tell what and how you learned? Should you add anything?
2. Could your friend tell the order in which things happened? Did you remember to use words like *first*, *next*, and *last*?
3. Did you write each part of your letter in the right place?
4. Did you use the right punctuation in sentences and the parts of your letter?
5. Now write your letter on another paper.

BUSTER'S JOB

Carol Carrick

While Kate liked to roller skate, Tony and Billy love to ice skate. These good friends have another friend who can't skate, but still likes to go with them. Buster, Billy's dog, shows the boys what a really good animal friend can do for you when you need help.

Billy listened hopefully for the hum of the bus while his parents waited in their truck. Tony was coming to spend the winter school break with Billy.

Every summer children from the city spent time with Billy's family in the country. It was fun for Billy because it was sometimes boring with no friends close by. Tony had stayed with them for the last two years. He returned because he was Billy's favorite. It was fun to share his room with someone he liked so much.

When Tony first came he must have been a tiny bit frightened because he never spoke to Billy's parents. When he did have something to say it was very softly and politely. Billy guessed that coming from the city streets, country life must seem a bit strange. And Tony was scared of even a tiny dog like Buster because he barked a lot.

"Buster wouldn't hurt anyone," Billy told him. "He thinks making noise is his job."

Tony got off the bus with a wide grin and a hug for everyone. At first it was fun just to share stories and be together again.

"Skating!" said Tony after breakfast one morning. "It's my favorite thing to do in winter. Can you skate around here?"

"We could try Green's Pond," said Billy.

"That's not a good idea," said Billy's father. "I have nothing against your skating, but that's a private pond. I don't think Mr. Green would want you there."

"Couldn't we call him," said Billy, "and ask very politely if we could skate there? We won't hurt anything."

"The ice isn't strong enough yet," his father said. "Maybe in a few days if it gets colder."

"But Tony will be gone by then."

Billy's father shook his head.

Billy and Tony just sat around all morning with nothing to do.

"This is boring," said Tony. "Let's go down and see how the ice looks."

"I guess there's nothing wrong with that," said Billy, "if we don't walk on it."

The boys and Buster soon came to the stand of trees where Mr. Green lived. On the fence was a sign that said PRIVATE. Cautiously, the two boys peeked from behind a bush to make sure nobody was around. Then they sneaked through the woods.

When they arrived at the pond they looked hopefully at the ice. The pond was almost round. In the middle was a place where the dark water showed through.

"My dad's right. It won't hold us yet,"
Billy whispered softly. He wasn't sure if
Mr. Green could hear them through the
woods. "Too bad," he sighed. "It would be
fun to go skating."

Just to see how strong it was, Tony
tossed a big rock across the ice. "I think
we could skate on this end," he said. He
began to walk on the ice, cautiously at
first, to try it out.

"My parents told us to stay off," said
Billy. "They're going to be mad."

"I don't care," said Tony. "They're not going to find out if you don't tell them."

Now Tony was almost to the middle. "Please come back," begged Billy. There was a creaking noise as the ice began to move a little. Then a loud crack.

"Watch out!" Billy yelled. But it was too late. It was strange how it happened so quickly. There was a scream and suddenly Tony was in the water.

Tony struggled to get out. He tried hanging on to the ice but as soon as he grabbed hold he would slip off again. Billy knew Tony couldn't stay in the water much longer.

Lying down, Billy began to push himself carefully out on the ice. He was very frightened, but he knew there was no time to go for help. Behind him Buster barked loudly. When Billy got as close as he could, he reached out to Tony, but his arm wasn't long enough. What would he do now?

"Come back, Billy," someone shouted. Mr. Green had heard Buster. As Billy cautiously returned, inch by inch, Mr. Green looked around for something long enough. He pulled on a dry branch, putting his whole body against it, until it cracked off. He got to Tony just in time and pulled him out.

Soon Mr. Green had Tony back at the house warming himself with hot soup. "It was a good thing Buster did his job," said Mr. Green. "He saved your life."

"Good dog," Tony said to Buster. "Thank goodness you know your job so well."

Thinking and Writing About the Selection

1. What was Tony's favorite thing to do in winter?

2. Why did Tony come to the country?

3. How did Buster save Tony's life?

4. If you were Billy, would you have gone out on the ice with Tony? Why or why not?

Applying the Key Skill
Best Title

Look back at "Buster's Job." Write a sentence that tells why this was a good title for the story. Now look at these titles for the same story. Which one do you like best and why?

a. Buster Can't Skate
b. Buster Saves Tony
c. Ice and Hot Soup

Mandy's Grandmother

Liesel Moak Skorpen

Tony was shy when he first met Billy
and his family. Sometimes it takes a while
to make a new friend. Mandy is going to meet
her grandmother for the first time. Mandy
thinks she knows all about grandmothers
because her picture book shows her one.
Mandy hopes her grandmother will be just
like the one in her book. But Mandy and
her grandmother find out that making friends
takes a bit of work.

Mandy's grandmother was coming for a visit.

Mandy had a picture book with a grandmother in the story. That grandmother took the little girl for walks and to the zoo. She had plenty of time to hold her on her lap. Mandy looked at all the pictures carefully, especially the ones with the girl on the grandmother's lap.

On the day that Mandy's grandmother was coming, Mandy had to clean her room, take a bath, and change her clothes.

Mandy put on clean jeans, her favorite sweater, and her floppy hat.

Mandy's grandmother came in a furry coat and a funny hat with flowers. She had an interesting box in her arms.

"And who is this little fellow?" she said to Mandy.

"Why, that's our Mandy," said Mandy's mother quickly.

"Oh, dear," said Mandy's grandmother, embarrassed. She was fumbling with her packages and trying to smile at Mandy.

"I can hardly wait to see Mandy in this," Mandy's grandmother said.

Maybe it's cowboy clothes, Mandy thought, tearing the ribbons off.

The dress was yellow. So was the hat. The purse had a little lace hanky inside. "Thank you," said Mandy softly but politely. She tried to smile but it came out crooked.

121

Mandy was sitting in her room looking through that grandmother book. She had a sign tacked to her door. It said: MANDY'S PRIVATE ROOM. PLEASE KNOCK! But her grandmother didn't.

"Show me your dolls," said Grandmother brightly. "How your mother used to love her dolls."

"I don't have dolls," said Mandy. "I don't like them. I have a frog, though," she said hopefully. "His name is Wart." Mandy lifted her hat and there was Wart sleeping on her head. Mandy's grandmother screamed, her mother came running, and Mandy was sent outside.

"What I know about grandmothers," Mandy said to Wart, "is that they're very boring, and that mine is mean and doesn't like me."

The next day Mandy's grandmother didn't come down.

"Take her up this cup of tea," Mandy's mother said.

"She doesn't like me," Mandy said.

"Of course she does," said Mandy's mother sternly. "She loves you."

Mandy knocked.

"Come in," said Mandy's grandmother softly.
Her grandmother was sitting by the window. Her
eyes were closed. Mandy set the tea on the table.
She was thinking about the picture book, because
she was feeling like sitting on somebody's lap.

"I brought some tea," said Mandy.

"Thank you, dear," Mandy's grandmother said,
"but I'm not feeling very well."

Mandy saw that her grandmother had been
crying. It made her stomach feel strange to think
about grownups crying.

"Tea's very good for you," Mandy said.

Mandy's grandmother closed her eyes again. She didn't take the tea.

"I think you must be very sad," said Mandy.

"I am a little sad," Mandy's grandmother said. "I was thinking about when your mother was little like you. I used to hold her on my lap."

"I like laps, too," said Mandy quickly. "I like laps a lot."

And Mandy's grandmother held out her arms and there was Mandy in her lap. Mandy's arms were around her neck and her face was pressed against her.

They had their breakfast together by the window. After breakfast Mandy showed her grandmother the barn.

She showed her grandmother the chickens and the goats and Strawberry Pony.

"Does he bite?" her grandmother asked.

"Not if he likes you," Mandy said.

Mandy's grandmother fed him carrot sticks and the pony licked her hand.

"Would you like to ride him?" Mandy asked.

Mandy's grandmother thought that she wouldn't.

Her grandmother took a good look at Wart, but she didn't want to hold him. "Friends don't have to share everything," she said. Mandy thought that over and decided she was right. They packed a lunch and ate it on the picnic rock up on the hill.

The next day they talked a lot. Mandy's grandmother told her stories of when her mother was a little girl. About how she once made cookies with salt instead of sugar and how she used to write poems for Grandfather's birthday and how she fell in her uncle's pond with her new hat on. Mandy told her grandmother a secret she had never told before.

Mandy's grandmother taught her how to knit. Mandy taught her grandmother how to whistle. In the evening they sat by the fire and whistled and knit.

It was time for Mandy's grandmother to go. They were sitting in the airport. She sat waiting for the airplane to come, smiling and knitting.

"I love you, Mandy," her grandmother said.

"I love you, too," said Mandy, because she did.

Thinking and Writing About the Selection

1. What did Mandy and her grandmother teach each other?

2. How do you know Mandy didn't like the things her grandmother gave her?

3. Why do you think Mandy's grandmother was sad?

4. Has anyone ever given you something you didn't like? How did you act?

Applying the Key Skill
Cause of an Event

Number your paper from 1 to 3. Finish each sentence about the story "Mandy's Grandmother."

1. Mandy had to take a bath, clean her room, and change her clothes because ____.

2. Mandy's grandmother did not come downstairs the next day so ____.

3. Mandy wanted to sit in her grandmother's lap because ____.

SKILLS activity

CAUSE OF AN EVENT

How can you tell why something has happened in a story? And how can you tell why someone does something? One way is to look for the words <u>because</u> and <u>so</u>. These words tell you the **cause** of an event. The cause is why it happened.

Read the stories. Think about the cause of the event, or why it happened. Then write the answer to each question on your paper. Use complete sentences.

ACTIVITY A Mandy has a pet frog and a pony because she likes animals. She also likes to share her pets with her friends. Mandy's grandmother is not used to animals, so she just looks at the animals when she visits Mandy. She doesn't hold the frog or ride the pony.

1. Why does Mandy have a frog and pony?
    a. Her grandmother gave them to her.
    b. She likes animals.
    c. She lives in the city.

2. Why does Mandy's grandmother just look at the animals?

   a. She isn't used to animals.

   b. She doesn't like to share with Mandy.

   c. She loves animals.

ACTIVITY B Dan lives near a pond that is frozen. He practices skating every day so he can be on the skating team. He gets up early so he can skate when it is light out. He can't skate when he gets home from school because it is too dark.

1. Why does Dan practice skating every day?

   a. He wants to keep warm.

   b. He wants to meet his friends.

   c. He wants to be on the skating team.

2. Why does Dan get up early to skate?

   a. He wants to skate when it is light out.

   b. He wants to skate alone.

   c. He wants to skate to school.

Toys Today
AND
YESTERDAY

Virginia Arnold

Mandy and her grandmother didn't
always think of the same kinds of toys for
a little girl. Did you ever see the toys your
grandparents may have played with? In this
story, you will find out about some very old
toys and some very new ones, too.

What kind of toys do you like to play with?
Do you like toys that are out of the ordinary? You
may think your favorite toy is different, but it may
have been around for quite a while.

Have you used roller skates to have some
fun? The first roller skates were a flat piece of
wood with the wheels made of wood, too. Those
first skates let the skater go rolling forward
without stopping. But the idea of roller skating
caught on and everybody wanted to do it. People
searched for a better kind of skate. Someone came
up with the idea of making skates that could turn.
Besides just going forward, the skater could make
interesting moves using the turning skates. The
skates that you use today let you turn and even
let you stop.

If some children didn't have roller skates, they may have made another toy on wheels. It was called the scooter. It was an ordinary toy that was easy and fun to make. The scooter had a board to stand on. Roller skate wheels were put on the bottom of the board. A long piece of wood coming up from the bottom board had two handles. The skater could hold on to the handles. He or she put one foot on the board while the other foot pushed along the sidewalk. This moved the skater along. Then, one day someone tried to ride on only the bottom board. Can you guess what toy was born? The skateboard!

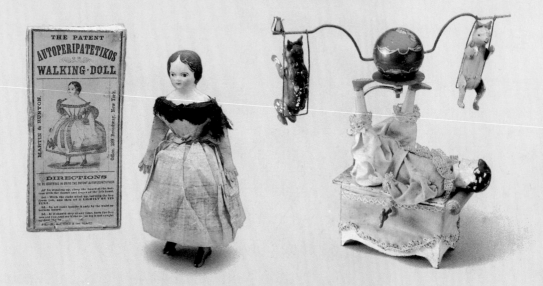

Maybe you have searched in a store that has
old mechanical toys. These toys may be over one
hundred years old. They are worth a lot of money.
There is a doll that walks when you wind a key
in its back. Other old wind-up toys have many
parts. One toy is a man in the circus making some
bears balance.

The idea of mechanical toys caught on and is
here to stay. Today, almost everybody likes to
play with toys that "do" things. Maybe you have
seen a toy car or truck that had lights that blinked
and blinked. Did the truck go forward and back,
fast and slow? Sometimes the truck might even
turn over!

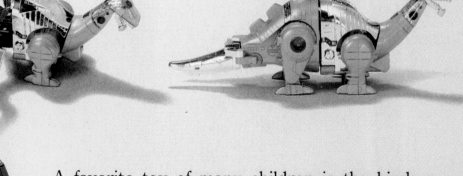

A favorite toy of many children is the kind that changes from one thing to another. First, the toy is a robot, then you turn some parts and you change the toy into a car. Turn some other parts and the car changes to an animal. How about a toy that changes from a robot to a dinosaur? If you have a toy that changes, you really have two toys for the price of one!

In this story, you have read how the toys of today are very much like the toys of yesterday. Children still play with toys on wheels and toys that move along. You have also read how the toys of today are different from the toys of yesterday. Some of today's toys move in a different way or change their parts. But you probably love toys the same way your grandma and grandpa did because—TOYS ARE FUN!

Thinking and Writing About the Selection

1. Tell how the toy scooter was made.

2. How are the roller skates of today different from the first kind of skates?

3. Why do you think that almost everybody likes to play with mechanical toys?

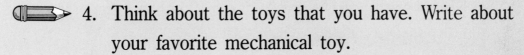 4. Think about the toys that you have. Write about your favorite mechanical toy.

Applying the Key Skill
Homophones

Read each sentence. Find the word that correctly completes the sentence. Then write the word on your paper.

1. Please put that new toy over ___.
   a. hear   b. here

2. This mechanical toy has an ___ that blinks.
   a. eye   b. I

3. The little toy doll has a ___ hat.
   a. blew   b. blue

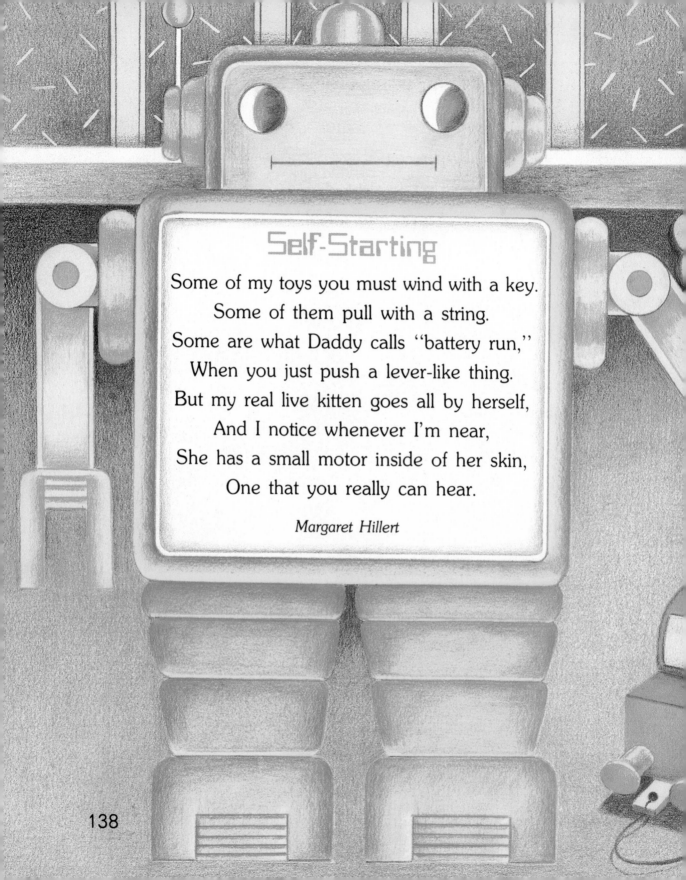

Self-Starting

Some of my toys you must wind with a key.
Some of them pull with a string.
Some are what Daddy calls "battery run,"
When you just push a lever-like thing.
But my real live kitten goes all by herself,
And I notice whenever I'm near,
She has a small motor inside of her skin,
One that you really can hear.

Margaret Hillert

138

139

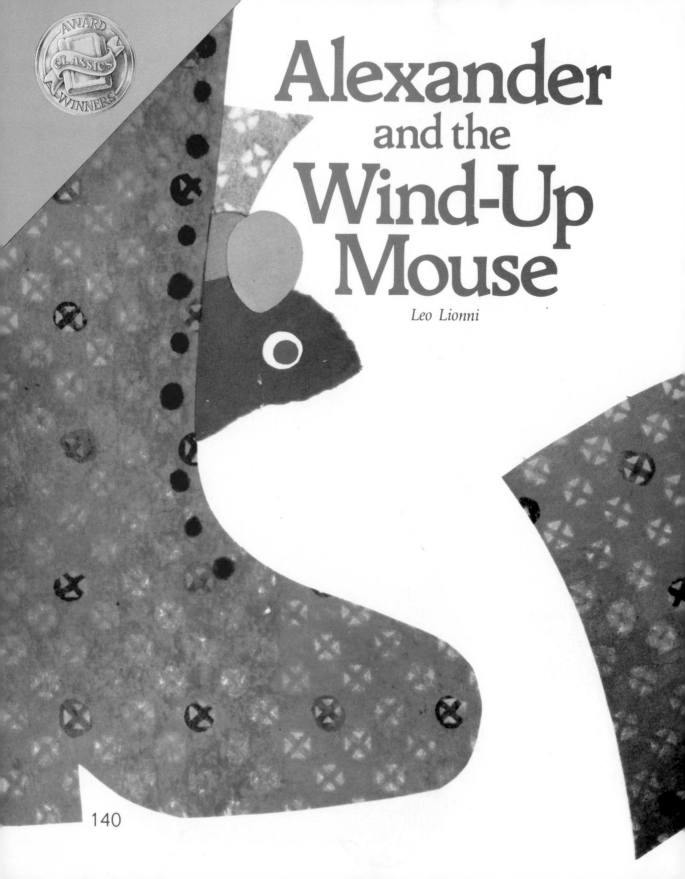

Alexander
and the
Wind-Up
Mouse

Leo Lionni

Many children have a favorite toy that they love. But as they get new toys, they may forget their poor favorite toy. Willy is about to have this happen to him when he gets to know Alexander. Alexander and Willy together learn what it means to be a true friend.

141

"Help! Help! A mouse!" There was a scream. Then a crash. Cups, saucers, and spoons were flying in all directions. Alexander ran for his hole as fast as his little legs would carry him. All Alexander wanted was a few crumbs and yet every time they saw him they would scream for help or chase him with a broom.

One day, when there was no one in the house, Alexander heard a squeak in Annie's room. He sneaked in and what did he see? Another mouse.

But not an ordinary mouse like himself. Instead of legs it had two little wheels, and on its back there was a key.

"Who are you?" asked Alexander.

143

"I am Willy the wind-up mouse, Annie's favorite toy. They wind me to make me run around in circles, they cuddle me, and at night I sleep on a soft white pillow between the doll and a woolly teddy bear. Everyone loves me."

"They don't care much for me," said Alexander sadly. But he was happy to have found a friend. "Let's go to the kitchen and look for crumbs," he said.

"Oh, I can't," said Willy. "I can only move when they wind me. But I don't mind. Everybody loves me."

Alexander, too, came to love Willy. He went to visit him whenever he could. He told him of his adventures with brooms, flying saucers, and mousetraps. Willy talked about the penguin, the woolly bear, and mostly about Annie. The two friends spent many happy hours together.

But when he was alone in the dark of his hideout, Alexander thought of Willy with envy.

"Ah!" he sighed. "Why can't I be a wind-up mouse like Willy and be cuddled and loved."

One day Willy told a strange story. "I've heard," he whispered mysteriously, "that in the garden, at the end of the pebble path, close to the blackberry bush, there lives a magic lizard who can change one animal into another."

"Do you mean," said Alexander, "that he could change me into a wind-up mouse like you?"

That very afternoon Alexander went into the garden and ran to the end of the path. "Lizard, lizard," he whispered. And suddenly there stood before him, full of the colors of flowers and butterflies, a large lizard. "Is it true that you could change me into a wind-up mouse?" asked Alexander in a quivering voice.

"When the moon is round," said the lizard, "bring me a purple pebble."

For days and days Alexander searched the garden for a purple pebble. In vain. He found yellow pebbles and blue pebbles and green pebbles—but not one tiny purple pebble.

At last, tired and hungry, he returned to the house. In a corner of the pantry he saw a box full of old toys, and there, between blocks and broken dolls, was Willy. "What happened?" said Alexander, surprised.

Willy told him a sad story. It had been Annie's birthday. There had been a party and everyone had brought a gift. "The next day," Willy sighed, "many of the old toys were put in this box. We will all be thrown away."

Alexander was almost in tears. "Poor, poor Willy!" he thought. But then suddenly something caught his eye. Could it really be . . . ? Yes it was! It was a little purple pebble.

All excited, he ran to the garden, the precious pebble tight in his arms. There was a full moon. Out of breath, Alexander stopped near the blackberry bush. "Lizard, lizard, in the bush," he called quickly. The leaves rustled and there stood the lizard. "The moon is round, the pebble found," said the lizard. "Who or what do you wish to be?"

"I want to be . . ." Alexander stopped. Then suddenly he said, "Lizard, lizard, could you change Willy into a mouse like me?" The lizard blinked. There was a blinding light. And then all was quiet. The purple pebble was gone.

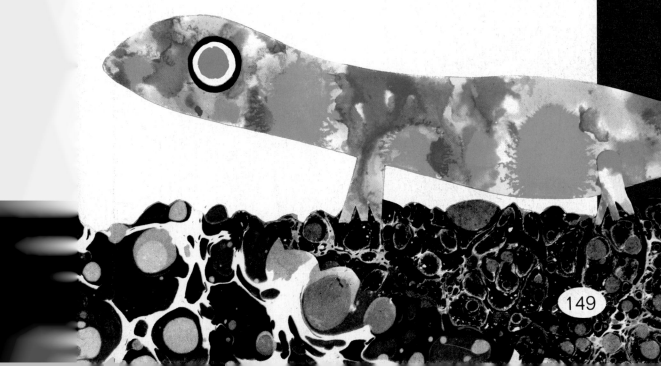

Alexander ran back to the house as fast as he could.

The box was there, but alas it was empty. "Too late," he thought, and with a heavy heart he went to his hole in the baseboard.

Something squeaked! Cautiously Alexander moved closer to the hole. There was a mouse inside. "Who are you?" said Alexander, a little frightened.

"My name is Willy," said the mouse.

"Willy!" cried Alexander. "The lizard . . . the lizard did it!" He hugged Willy and then they ran to the garden path. And there they danced until dawn.

Thinking and Writing About the Selection

1. What did the lizard say Alexander should bring him?

2. Why did Alexander want to be like Willy?

3. Why do you think Alexander made a good wish?

 4. If you could have any wish, what would it be?

Applying the Key Skill
Long Vowels

Number your paper from 1 to 5. Look at the underlined letters in each key word. Then find the word in the row that has the same vowel sound. Write that word on your paper.

1. boot   a. foot   b. floor   c. flute   d. money

2. hope   a. stop   b. boat   c. some   d. soon

3. blow   a. from   b. owls   c. should   d. show

4. flew   a. shook   b. own   c. blue   d. also

5. huge   a. music   b. jungle   c. hug   d. buses

Caring

In *Caring*, you read about some people who cared about each other. Some of the stories like "Blueberries for Sal" and "Skating for a Gold Medal" told about families and how they cared for each other. Other stories like "My Friend Jacob" and "Buster's Job" told about how friends care. If you care about someone, you just might find that you feel good about yourself, too.

Thinking and Writing About *Caring*

1. How did Theodore's friends in "That's What Friends Are For" and the Bremen Town musicians work together?

2. How did Carmela in "A Gift for Tía Rosa" and Sammy in "My Friend Jacob" show that they cared about someone?

3. Why did Alexander in "Alexander and the Wind-Up Mouse" decide to change his wish and let Willy become a live mouse?

4. Why do you think Mandy's grandmother cared about how Mandy felt about her?

 5. Write about a friend, a pet, or someone in your family that you care about.

Introducing Level 7

SOARING

The stories in this unit are all about flying. You will read about real and imaginary flights into space. You will also read about people who fly airplanes, soar in balloons, and fly kites. What is your favorite way to fly?

Somewhere over the rainbow
Bluebirds fly.
Birds fly over the rainbow—
Why then, oh why can't I?

Edgar Y. Harburg
"Over the Rainbow"
The Wizard of Oz

153

Ezra Jack Keats

REGARDS
TO THE
MAN
IN THE
MOON

Flying is very ordinary to people today.
In fact, when you grow up, a trip to the
moon may be as ordinary as a trip in
your family car. Certainly, you can
always use your imagination to
take you to wondrous places.
Louie and Susie use their
imagination to fly right out
of the world. What strange
adventures wait for them?

"What's up, Louie—why so sad?" Barney asked.

"The kids are laughing at me."

"Laughing at you—why?"

"Well—"

"Come on, you can tell me. I'm your Pop now."

"Well," Louie said, "they call you the junkman."

"Junk?" Barney growled. "They should know better than to call this junk. All a person needs is some imagination! And a little of that stuff can take you right out of this world. What do you say, Louie, want to give it a try?"

Louie and his parents got to work.

"What's going on?" the kids asked.

"I'm going out of this world," Louie answered.

The kids snickered and nudged each other. "Is that *Voyager III*?" they laughed.

"No," he said, "It's *IMAGINATION I*!"

"Well, don't run out of gas!"

"Regards to the Man in the Moon," they kidded.

156

"Are you going out there all alone?" Susie asked. "Can I come with you, Louie? Can I?"

"Well, that depends—got lots of imagination?" he asked.

"Oh yes," she said. "And—and I'll bring cookies, too!"

"Hmm, okay, be here early tomorrow."

The next morning they climbed aboard. "Ready when you are," Susie shouted.

"Okay then," yelled Louie. "Blast off!" They held their breath.

BAARROOOMMM!

Way out in space they opened their eyes. "We did it!" Susie gasped. They stared down at planet Earth. "Everybody we know is down there—and we're all alone up here. I'm scared."

"Me too!" Louie whispered.

They floated past strange and wondrous things . . . and on through worlds no one had ever seen before.

Suddenly they were jolted to a halt. "Help! Help us!" they heard familiar voices cry. It was Ziggie and Ruthie.

"We decided to follow you," Ziggie
cried, "but we've used all our imagination.
We're stuck. We can't move. Don't untie
us, please, or we'll never get home."

"Let go!" Susie yelled. "Or we'll all be
stuck out here forever. You can only move
on your own imagination!"

"Let go, will you," Louie cried. "There's a rock storm heading this way. We'll be smashed to bits!"

"They're not rocks! Can't you see? They're monsters!" Ziggie moaned. "They're coming to capture us. We'll never see home again!"

"Monsters!" Susie said. "Now you're using your imagination." They began to move. "You're doing fine now," Susie called. "So let go! You'll do better on your own and so will we." But Ziggie and Ruthie were so scared they just hung on.

They ducked this way—and that—and over—and under—and upside down.

Finally the storm passed and they headed for home. "Wow!" Ziggie joked nervously. "Wasn't that fun?"

"Yeah, we sure scared those monsters!" Ruthie bragged. "Wish we could do it again!"

"And they thought," Louie said, "they used up their imagination!"

They were getting close to home when Ziggie finally dropped the rope.

Next day they told everybody about their adventures. Soon all the kids were ready to take off.

Thinking and Writing About the Selection

1. Why did the kids laugh at Louie?

2. How did Louie's father show what you could do with a little imagination?

3. Why do you think Louie's spaceship could move only on imagination?

 4. If you could use your imagination to go anywhere, where would you like to go?

Applying the Key Skill
Character's Motives or Feelings

Use complete sentences to answer these questions about some of the characters in "Regards to the Man in the Moon."

1. Why is Louie sad at the beginning of the story?

2. Why do you think Louie wants to show the other kids what you can do with a little imagination?

3. Why are Ziggie and Ruthie frightened after they go into "space"?

163

Ezra Jack Keats

Ezra Jack Keats was an artist and writer for over 30 years. He died in 1983.

In stories like *A Snowy Day*, readers feel they know the character Peter well. Keats' style is to tell his stories as simply as possible. In this way, the reader can add his or her own experiences to the story.

Keats began drawing when he was four years old. He never took a real art lesson in his life. As an adult, Keats decided to become an illustrator. After doing art for other people's books for ten years, he started to write his own stories.

More to Read
The Snowy Day,
A Letter to Amy,
Hi, Cat!

TIRED OLD WORDS

I got my hair cut. Do you like it?

It looks nice.

It looks OK.

It's a nice haircut.

Your hair looks beautiful!

Sometimes when we speak or write, we use the same words over and over. Read the paragraph with tired words. Then find a word in the box that is more exciting. Write the new paragraph on your paper.

When Susie and Louie climbed <u>on</u> *Imagination I* the kids <u>laughed</u> and <u>pushed</u> each other. "<u>Give our best</u> to the Man in the Moon," they kidded. But out in space, Susie and Louie looked at all the <u>nice</u> things. They couldn't wait to tell the other kids about their <u>ride</u>.

wondrous	nudged	aboard
Regards	giggled	adventure

HARRIET
AND
WILLIAM

AND THE
TERRIBLE
CREATURE

Valerie Scho Carey
Illustrated by Lynne Cherry

Louie and his friends liked their flying trip on **Imagination I.** *Some people just don't like adventures. Harriet likes traveling, but her brother, William, doesn't. When Harriet makes a spaceship, will she be able to talk William into coming with her into space? What strange adventures do you think they may have?*

Harriet and William were twins. Harriet liked going places. William liked working in his garden.

The day Harriet finished building her spaceship, she said, "Let's go on a trip."

"No, thank you," said William.

"Why not?" asked Harriet.

"Because I could not sleep in a spaceship. I can only sleep in my own bed."

"You can't take your bed with you. It's a very small ship," said Harriet. "But you can take your pillow. Now will you come?"

"No," said William.

"Why not?" asked Harriet.

"I would rather stay home and take care of my garden," William said.

"All right," said Harriet. "Good-bye for now."

Va-ROOM went the spaceship. It took off into the sky with Harriet alone inside. Harriet was pushed against her seat as the spaceship went faster and faster.

"I wish William had come," she said to herself.

She passed the moon and all the planets. "Time for some exercise," thought Harriet. She was just unbuckling her seat belt when—

Crash!

The spaceship had landed. Harriet climbed out. "Rocks and stumps. Stumps and lumps," she said. "William would not like this at all."

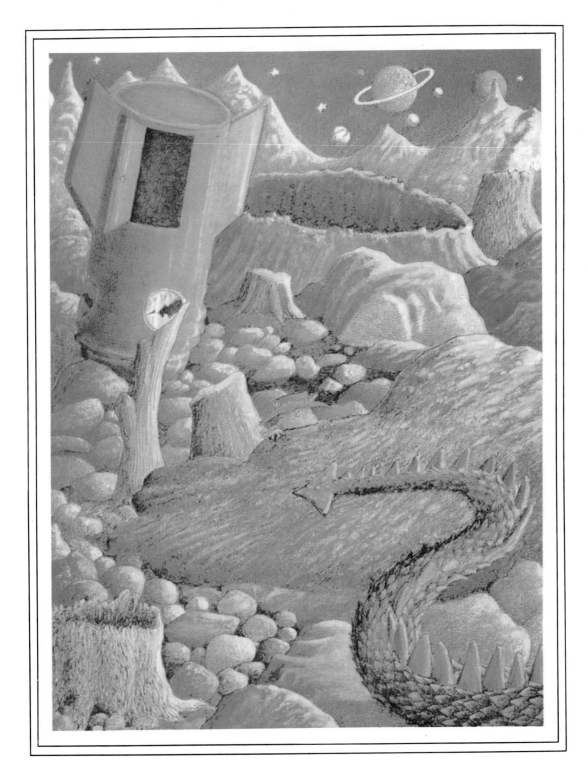

169

Crunch.

Harriet jumped.

Crunch and *munch.*

Harriet hid behind a rock.

Crunch. Munch. Smunch.

Harriet peeked around the rock. There was a TERRIBLE CREATURE, a dragonish thing. It had buggly eyes, a big snorting nose, and two webbed wings. And it had a mouth full of rocks. It was chewing rocks up. It was spitting rocks out.

"Oh my. Oh me," cried the creature. Big tears fell from its buggly eyes.

Harriet felt sorry for it. "Even dragonish things must have feelings," she thought. "Why are you crying?" she asked.

"You would cry too if you had to eat rocks," it said.

"Then why do you eat them?"

"Because all the flowers are gone. I ate them all. Then I ate all the trees. Now I am eating rocks because there is nothing else."

"Would you eat a Harriet if you saw one?" asked Harriet.

"Is Harriet a flower, a tree, or a rock?" asked the creature.

"None of those," said Harriet.

"Then I would not eat one."

"Good," said Harriet, and she came out from behind the rock.

"Why don't you grow some flowers?" she asked.

"I don't know how," sobbed the creature. Big tears spattered on the rocks. Harriet handed it her handkerchief.

"I have an idea," she said. "I will help you if you will help me."

Harriet showed the creature her spaceship. "If I can just get it to fly again, I can go home and see my brother, William. He knows all about growing flowers. I am sure he would know what to do."

"I would like to help you, but I don't know anything about spaceships." The creature began to cry again.

"Don't worry about that." Harriet patted the creature, then got out her tools, and went to work.

At last she called the dragonish thing over. "Get behind the ship and blow as hard as you can. Just be careful not to blow fire."

The thing sucked in a big breath and *poof* let it out. Nothing happened. It sucked in a bigger breath. *Va-ROOM*. The ship lifted off the ground and into space.

174

Squish. The ship landed on William's tomatoes.

"They will never be the same," said William, "but I am glad you are safe at home. I missed you."

Harriet hugged William. "I missed you, too."

She told him all about her trip and the dragonish thing. "William, will you please help?"

William frowned.

"Just this once, couldn't you please come along? You know so much more about planting gardens than I do."

William thought about leaving his garden with no one to take care of it. He thought about Harriet going alone. What if her spaceship crashed again? She could be stuck forever on that lumpy planet, with nothing to eat but rocks.

"I'll go," said William.

Harriet fixed her ship. William collected his garden tools and seeds.

Harriet and William flew past the moon and all the planets. Harriet steered the ship straight to the terrible creature's home.

"I was afraid you would not come," it said.

"A promise is a promise," said Harriet.

The three worked hard to make a garden. William knew just what to do. They carried away rocks. They dug a well for water. They shoveled and raked the ground to make a flower bed.

At last the garden was planted.

"Thank you," said the terrible creature and it began to cry.

"Why are you crying now?" asked Harriet. "Did we forget something?"

"No," sniffled the creature. "But now you will be going home, and I will miss you."

"Please don't cry," said William. "We will come again."

Harriet was proud of her brother. "I'm glad you said that. Traveling is not really so bad, is it?"

But William did not answer.

"What are you doing?" asked William one day.

"I am building a boat," said Harriet. "I am going to sail around the world. Will you come with me?"

"No, thank you," said William, and he went on weeding his garden.

Thinking and Writing About the Selection

1. Why didn't William want to go with Harriet in her spaceship?

2. Why did Harriet ask the terrible creature if he would eat a Harriet?

3. Why do you think Harriet wished William had come with her after she took off?

4. Where would you like to go with Harriet on her boat trip?

Applying the Key Skill
Possessive Nouns

Read each pair of sentences. Find the sentence that tells about somebody owning something. Write it on your paper.

1. a. Harriet wants to go on a trip.
   b. Harriet's spaceship is very small.

2. a. The ship landed on William's tomatoes.
   b. Harriet gave the creature a handkerchief.

I CAN FLY

I can fly, of course,
Very low,
Not fast,
Rather slow,

I spread my arms
Like wings,
Lean on the wind,
And my body zings
About.
Nothing showy—
A few loops
And turns—
But for the most
Part,
I just coast.

However,
Since people are prone
To talk about
It,
I generally prefer,
Unless I am alone,
Just to walk about.

Felice Holman

181

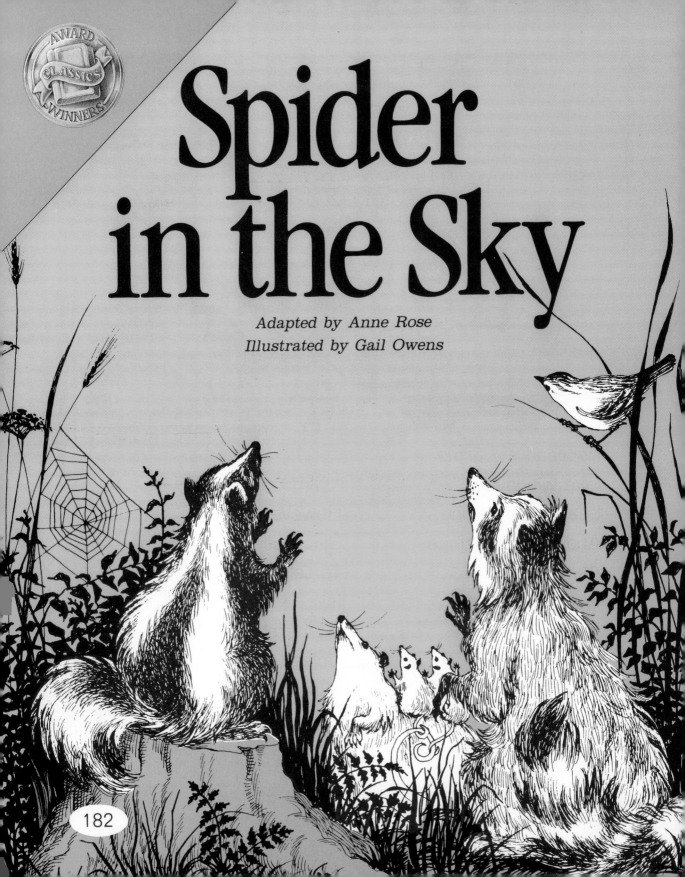

Spider in the Sky

Adapted by Anne Rose
Illustrated by Gail Owens

Who would have thought that Harriet and William could help such a big creature? It doesn't matter how little you are, if you know what to do. A wise little spider knows just how to help her friends, and she takes her own trip into space to do it.

Back in the long ago, the animals had no heat or light. They felt around in the dark and shivered from cold.

"What we need is fire and light," Coyote said.

"Fire and light is what we need," Raven agreed.

A meeting was called, but it was so dark that some of the animals lost their way. They haven't been found to this day.

When there was enough noise, the meeting was called to order. "There is such a thing as fire and light. It's called the sun," Jackal said. "It's on the other side of the mountain."

"Let's get it," cried the animals.

"Trouble is," Jackal went on, "those who have the sun won't part with it."

"We'll take it from them," the animals yelled.

Finally Skunk was elected to go because he could hide the sun in his thick furry tail.

As Skunk got closer and closer to the sun, it grew hotter and brighter, but he kept going. At long last he came to the other side of the mountain. There he found the sun. Quickly, quickly, he snapped off a piece of the sun. Then he hid it in his tail. But the sun slid down his tail and escaped.

"Too bad," the animals said when poor
Skunk came back with a white stripe down
his bushy tail. And still it was cold, and dark.

"Now it's my turn to go," Eagle said.
"I'll hide the sun on my head." So Eagle
flew off, going east as Skunk had. Since
eagles soar high, no one saw him dive
straight down out of the sky. Swiftly,
swiftly, he grabbed a piece of the sun. He
placed it on his head and flew off. But the
sun was so hot, it burned a hole right
through his feathers and escaped.

"Too bad," said the animals when poor Eagle returned with a bald head. And still it was cold and dark.

"A small creature could do this," a tiny voice said from the grass.

Everyone spoke up at once. "What? What? Who said that? What was that thin voice?"

"I am Grandmother Spider," a little spider said. "I will bring the sun's light and heat to you."

By the time the animals had stopped laughing, Grandmother Spider was on her way. Tied behind her web was a small pot of clay. Spinning a silver thread as she went, she, too, set off toward the east. So fast and quiet was she that no one saw her as she neared the sun. She was so little, so very little. All she needed was just a tiny piece of the sun. She reached out. Lightly, lightly, she tweaked a piece of the sun into her pot of clay. Her job done, she turned for home. She carefully followed the silver thread she herself had spun.

As she traveled, the sun's heat and light came before her. Wider and brighter it grew as sunshine does when it moves from east to west. And that's how back in the long ago, fire and light came to the animals.

Thinking and Writing About the Selection

1. Why had the animals felt around in the cold and dark?

2. Why weren't Skunk and Eagle able to bring the sun back to the animals?

3. Why do you think all the other animals laughed when Grandmother Spider said she would bring the sun to them?

 4. If you were one of the animals, what would you have done to get a piece of the sun?

Applying the Key Skill
Draw Conclusions

Use complete sentences to answer these questions about "Spider in the Sky."

1. When Grandmother Spider went to find the sun, why did she spin a silver thread as she set off toward the east?

2. Why couldn't anyone see Grandmother Spider as she neared the sun?

DRAW CONCLUSIONS

Sometimes an author does not tell you everything that happens in a story. Instead, you have to figure out for yourself what happens. You have to **draw conclusions** based on what is in the story and what you know could really happen.

Read the stories. Answer the questions on your paper about what happened. Then answer the question about how you were able to draw that conclusion.

ACTIVITY A Harriet was planting seeds in the garden. She planted seeds every day but nothing grew. She put each seed in the dirt. Then she walked to the house to get some water. When she came back, she saw four birds pecking in the dirt. "Go away!" Harriet called. "Look someplace else for dinner!"

1. Why didn't Harriet's seeds grow?
   a. She forgot to water them.
   b. Birds were flying away with them.
   c. Birds were eating them.

190

2. You know what happened because:

    a. Harriet saw the birds pecking at the seeds.

    b. Harriet put too much water on the seeds.

    c. The birds were flying with seeds in their mouths.

ACTIVITY B When Skunk got close to the hot sun, he had to squint. He snapped off a piece of the sun and hid it in his tail. But the sun slid down his tail and escaped. When Skunk came back, all he had was a white streak down his black tail.

1. What happened to Skunk's tail?

    a. The sun burned it off.

    b. The heat and light of the sun turned it white.

    c. Skunk left it with the sun.

2. You know what happened because:

    a. The sun slid down Skunk's tail.

    b. The sun hurt Skunk's eyes.

    c. The sun escaped.

191

What's in Space?

Susan Renner-Smith

Long ago, when people first told the story of "Spider in the Sky," they didn't know what they would find if they flew up into the sky. From the earth, they could see only the sun, the moon, and the stars.

But were there other things in the sky? Today we know there are more things in space. Read to find out some of the things we know about.

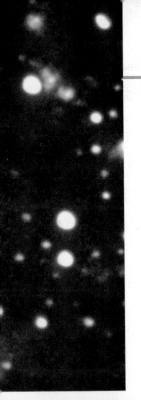

Do you ever go outside at night to see the sky? How many stars can you see? Try to count them. Do you think you can count them all?

The best way to see the stars is to ride in a rocket ship. You could go sailing up into the black and silent night. Higher and higher you would go. Soon you could look down on the earth below. You would be in space!

You may really do this one day. Many people have already gone into space on rocket ships. The rocket ships carried the people high into space. The earth looked like a giant ball to them. It just seemed to sit in space without moving.

The earth is not really motionless. The earth is a planet. A planet moves through space. It goes around the sun.

Our sun has eight other planets that orbit or go around it. The names of the planets are Mercury, Venus, Mars, Jupiter, Saturn, Uranus, Neptune, and Pluto.

Scientists have found other things in space. Many rocks, called asteroids, orbit the sun. You can't see asteroids even at night. They are too small.

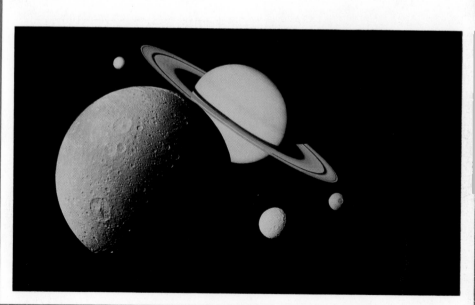

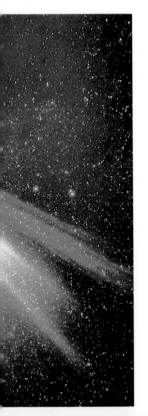

Comets are also in space. Most of the time, you can't see them either. A comet is a small world made of rock and ice. It has a long tail. We are just finding out about the tails of comets. A comet will orbit the sun, but it takes a strange path. Sometimes its path takes the comet far away from the sun. Other times it comes very close to the earth. Then we may see the comet.

Earth's Neighbors

Can we visit planets, asteroids, and comets? Not yet, but maybe one day we can. Scientists have sent more than one rocket to the planets. They have not sent any people yet.

People *have* made a visit to a very close neighbor in space. This neighbor is the moon. Some planets have many moons, but the earth has only one.

195

How close is the moon? You could fly to the moon in your rocket ship. You would finish the flight in only four days.

The moon is not the only thing that goes around the earth. Do you know what else can be found in space? There are many satellites in orbit around the earth. Each one is like a small spaceship. These satellites are not big enough to hold people.

How do the satellites get into space? Some satellites are sent by rocket. The space shuttle has carried many into space. As you know, the shuttle is a spaceship. Maybe you have seen the shuttle leave on one of its many trips.

The satellites have a big job to do. Some of them stay close to the earth. They are weather satellites that take pictures of the earth. The pictures help weather people tell us what the weather is and what it will be.

Other kinds of satellites are very high up in space. They seem to sit motionless over one place on the earth. These satellites send telephone calls from city to city. Your telephone might be silent for days if these satellites broke down.

The Stars

What do we know about the stars? There is only one star close to the earth. You can't see it in the night sky. This star is our sun.

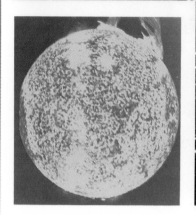

All stars are giant worlds of fire. Our sun is a giant world of fire. The stars in the night sky look very small. They look small because they are very far away.

People have not had a chance to visit a star. At this time no rocket is fast enough to go to the stars in one lifetime. Even with a faster rocket ship, it would take at least five years to get to the nearest star.

Does each star have its own planets like our sun? Do people live on the planets? There are many things we don't know about the stars. Many people look for answers every day. Maybe you will be the person to find those answers.

Thinking and Writing About the Selection

1. What is a comet?

2. Why can't we travel to the stars?

3. Why do you think people want to know more about space?

4. If you could go into space, where would you go? Why would you want to go there?

Applying the Key Skill
Antonyms

Read each sentence. Write the word that means the *opposite* of the underlined word.

1. Comets are <u>small</u> worlds made of rock and ice and orbit the sun.
   a. little   b. large   c. quiet

2. The stars you see at night are <u>far</u> away.
   a. close   b. big   c. huge

3. Rocket ships can carry people very high <u>up</u> into the sky.
   a. around   b. go   c. down

EARTH, MOON, AND SUN

While the earth spins on,
Turning, turning
Toward the sun,

The moon floats by
In its circle
In our sky.

And while it floats,
Earth and moon, two in one,
Rush on
With the bright planets
In a ring
Around the sun.

And as they rush
And swing
And turn
The gases of the sun
Swirl
And burn.

Claudia Lewis

The Adventure of Theo, Space Cowboy

Gibbs Davis

You have read about some of the things scientists know are in space. Theo and Sarah live in the future and are also very much interested in space. Join them as they take a high-flying adventure into space.

It was just the kind of afternoon Theo loved. Quiet.

He stared at the cover of his favorite book—MIKE SILVER, SPACE COWBOY. He must have read it a hundred times.

Theo knew the first sentence by heart. He closed his eyes and said it out loud.

"'It was no accident that Mike Silver was born on the day Zud took over the planet Earth.'"

Theo couldn't wait for Mike Silver to grow up and blast the horrible Zud into orbit.

"Theo!"

Oh no. It sounded like his mother's voice. Theo ducked under the covers. He suspected she wanted help with something.

Whatever it was would have to wait. Theo read on—Mike Silver had a horrible accident! His wings were on fire. Mike's spaceship just lost all power. He was headed toward some asteroids!

"Theo."

Theo's mother looked over the top of his book. "Didn't you hear me?"

Theo sighed. He just didn't hear well when he was reading.

"Sarah's mother just called. She has to work today. She's leaving Sarah with us for the afternoon."

Theo moaned. "Again?"

Sarah was always running around. She could get excited about any silly idea. He would never get in any reading today. Nuts.

"I guess you want me to play with her?" said Theo.

"It's just one afternoon," said Theo's mother. "How horrible could it be?"

Later that afternoon Sarah popped into the house yelling for Theo. "Come on, Theo." Sarah pulled Theo's book out of his hands. "I need a passenger."

"A passenger for what?" asked Theo.

"A passenger for the first flight of my wondrous spaceship. To tell the truth, Theo, I don't want to blast off alone the first time."

"No," said Theo. "I won't go with you." Theo took back his book.

"Chicken."

"There you go daring me again. It isn't my fault you made some silly spaceship you can't fly alone."

"Please, Theo. All you have to do is sit in the passenger seat. Don't be afraid."

"Who's afraid?" That did it! Theo put down his book. He followed Sarah to the door. "Just this once. But I'm warning you. After we play spaceship I want to be left alone to read. And no more daring."

Theo pulled the front door open and then gasped. He stared up and then up some more! He couldn't believe his eyes. Standing before him was a giant spaceship. It was part rocket and part car.

"Meet Star Car," said Sarah. "Come in for the ride of your life."

Theo quietly took the passenger seat. He didn't know what to expect next. Theo looked at Sarah. She sat by a computer.

Sarah stared out a window. "Door closed! Wings up!" She fired up the engine. "Hold onto your hat!"

Star Car soared up and up, a tail of flames behind her. For the first time, Theo forgot all about Mike Silver. He was too busy with his own adventure.

Star Car went roaring past flashing stars. They did circles around the moon. Sarah rode her ship like a true space cowboy.

Suddenly a warning light went on.

"We need some junk," said Sarah.

"You mean gas, don't you?"

"No, I don't," said Sarah. "Star Car runs on junk. We'll coast to the next planet."

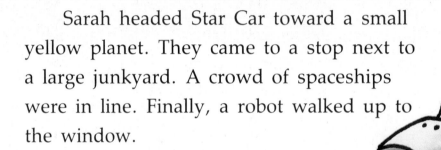

Sarah headed Star Car toward a small yellow planet. They came to a stop next to a large junkyard. A crowd of spaceships were in line. Finally, a robot walked up to the window.

"Hi, Spark," said Sarah.

"Where are you flying today?" The robot began to put junk into Star Car.

"Just out for a Saturday afternoon spin."

Sarah whispered, "He's very proud of his planet. Say something nice."

"Nice planet," said Theo, his voice cracking. He had never talked to a robot. Others were landing for junk.

"More business," said Spark. "Good-bye."

"Blast off!" said Sarah. Almost as soon as they were up in the air, the warning light went on again.

A hundred comets were heading straight toward them!

"I guess you know what to do," said Theo.

"I'm open for ideas."

Theo had to think fast. What would Mike Silver do? "Cut the power!" he shouted.

Sarah turned off the engine. Star Car dropped through the air. The comets overshot them by a foot.

Sarah took a deep breath. "How did you know what to do?"

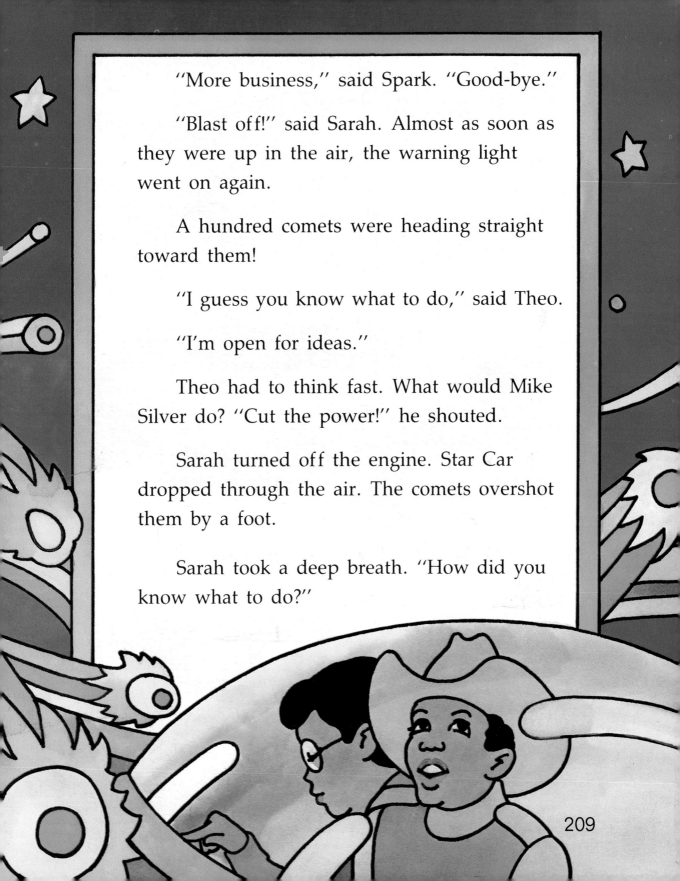

209

Theo shrugged. "I read it in a book."

"Can I borrow it sometime?" Sarah headed back to Earth.

"Sure thing!" said Theo.

It was just the kind of afternoon Theo loved. Quiet. As he reached for his milk, two books crashed to the floor.

"Sh!" said Sarah.

"Look who's wanting quiet," laughed Theo.

"Quiet!" Sarah looked over the top of MIKE SILVER, SPACE COWBOY. "Mike Silver is about to blast the horrible Zud into orbit."

"That's one of the best parts," said Theo. "Let's read it together!"

Thinking and Writing About the Selection

1. What was the name of Theo's favorite book?

2. Why did Theo know the first sentence of his favorite book?

3. Why do you think Sarah wanted to read Theo's book?

4. Write about one of your favorite books and why it means so much to you.

Applying the Key Skill
Main Idea

Read the story. Then answer the questions below. Write the answers on your paper.

> Sarah loved Theo's book *Mike Silver, Space Cowboy*. Theo read it with her after their space trip, and then he put it on the desk in his room. A few days later, Sarah visited Theo again. The first place she went was to Theo's desk.

1. What sentence tells the main idea?

2. Where did Sarah go when she got to Theo's?

WRITING activity

DESCRIPTIVE PARAGRAPH

Prewrite

In the story, "Regards to the Man in the Moon," Louie and Susie used their imagination to take a trip into space. Theo took a trip in Sarah's spaceship in "The Adventure of Theo, Space Cowboy." If you had a chance to go into space, would you go?

Pretend that you have been asked to be the first child to go into space on the space shuttle. The newspaper in your town asks you to write a paragraph telling why you want to be a passenger on the shuttle.

Before you write, you need to do some thinking. Why do you want to go? Do you want to see how the earth and moon look in space? Do you want to see a weather satellite?

Make a list of all your reasons for wanting to go into space. Look at the stories in *Soaring* for ideas. Talk with your friends about ideas, too.

Write

1. Pick three or four of the best ideas from your list.
2. Your first sentence can begin like this: I want to ride on the space shuttle because . . .
3. Write sentences that tell your other ideas.
4. Try to use Vocabulary Treasures in your paragraph.
5. Write a title for your paragraph.

Vocabulary Treasures	
adventure	silent
daring	wondrous

Revise

Read your paragraph again. Have a friend read it, too. Think about these ideas as you revise.

1. Could someone reading your paragraph find three or four ideas that tell why you want to go into space? If not, what sentences in your paragraph should you change?
2. Did you use some adjectives that would make your paragraph more interesting?
3. Did you use the correct punctuation in your sentences?
4. Now write your paragraph on another paper.

AMELIA'S FLYING MACHINE

Barbara Shook Hazen

Through the years, brave people with imagination have worked to learn about flying. One of those people was Amelia Earhart.

Once when she was little, Amelia wanted to show her friend Jimmy that she was not scared of anything. With the help of her cousins Katherine and Lucy and her sister Muriel, she made a roller coaster out of orange crates and some boards. On her first try, her car flipped over and Amelia fell on the ground. Amelia made the track longer, and now she is ready to try again.

"It looks okay," said Amelia, standing back. "Let's just hope it works this time."

"And hope Grandma Otis doesn't spoil everything," added Lucy. "She said she was going to take a nap. She sounded suspicious. She wanted to know what we were up to and why I had so many scratches."

"If Grandma decides to come out here, you're a goner," said Katherine.

"Well, my trip to Chicago is," said Amelia. "My father said I could go to Chicago with him to see the World's Fair if he gets a good report from Grandma. She thinks girls should only play with dolls."

Muriel's eyes grew big. "What are you going to do, Meeley?"

"Hope Jimmy comes over soon and hope Grandma takes that nap," said Amelia crossing her fingers.

Jimmy came over soon. "I wouldn't miss this for anything," he said with a grin.

Amelia made a face at him. Then she turned to the others. Once more she asked, "Shall we draw straws to see who goes first?"

"Not me," said Katherine. "Not after last time."

"Don't look at me," said Lucy.

Muriel shook her head. "Not me, Meeley," she said. "But if you go, I'll keep my fingers crossed."

"See," said Jimmy. "Didn't I tell you so! All of them are scared silly! I'll bet you are too. Only you're too stubborn to admit it. Girls are scaredy cats."

Amelia stamped her foot. "That's not so," she said. "I'm not scared. Just you watch."

Once again she carried the orange crate up
the ladder to the hayloft. She climbed into the car.
Then she pushed herself halfway out of the hayloft
window. There she waited and took a deep breath.
"It's got to work," she whispered to herself. "It's
just got to."

"What are you waiting for?" teased Jimmy.
"Santa Claus? Or me to try it for you?"

Amelia glared at Jimmy.

"Don't listen to him," yelled Lucy.

"Don't do it," said Katherine under her breath.

Muriel turned her head. She crossed as many fingers as she could. She closed her eyes tight. She didn't want to watch.

But she did want to see what was going on. When she opened her eyes to peek, she looked up and screamed, "Stop, Meeley! You can't go!"

The warning came too late. Amelia had just let go. The car started to roll. As it picked up speed, it went faster and faster down the long track.

Amelia felt the speed and the wind in her face. "Wow! Look at me," she cried out. "I'm really flying!"

The orange crate kept going. It rolled to the
end of the track, and then onto the ground. Amelia
waved and grinned at Jimmy as she went by. He
grinned back at her.

The car finally came to a stop—right by a
pair of black-stockinged feet.

"Oh-oh," said Amelia looking up.

Grandmother Otis stared down at Amelia. Her
hands were on her hips.

She spoke in her slow we'll-get-to-the-
bottom-of-this voice. "Amelia Mary, what are you
up to? And what kind of fool contraption is this? I
guessed something. And I guess your father will
have something to say when he hears about it."

Grandmother Otis tapped her foot. "Young
lady, was all this your idea?" she asked. "Or did
someone put you up to it?"

Amelia groaned. Telling the truth meant
missing Chicago and the Fair and going with her
father and everything.

"Yes, Gram," she said in a small voice. "It was all my idea." Then she sighed deeply.

Grandma Otis sighed, too. "Amelia Mary, I don't know whatever will become of you if you don't . . ."

"Ma'am," Jimmy interrupted, "it really wasn't Amelia's fault. I mean, she made it and rode on it. But I guess I kind of put her up to it."

Grandmother Otis turned toward Jimmy. "I might have thought so," she said. "I didn't think any granddaughter of mine could do such a silly thing."

She shook her finger at Jimmy. "Yes, I should have known you were behind this, Jimmy Watson. You have a habit of getting my girls in trouble. Why I have half a mind . . ."

Amelia jumped to her feet. "But, but, Grandma. Jimmy's not to blame. I'm the one who . . ."

"I don't want to listen," said Grandma Otis sternly. She picked up her skirts. "Amelia, Muriel. Girls. Come with me," she ordered.

"As for you, young man," she looked hard at Jimmy, "You stay right here and take down this contraption. Right now. Break it up, every bit of it, mind you." She turned on her heels and headed for the house.

Amelia hung back. "It isn't fair," she said to Jimmy. "You're getting the blame. It was my idea."

"So what!" Jimmy shrugged. "She'll get over it. You'll get to go to Chicago. She never tells my pa, and she won't tell yours either."

"Do you know something?" Amelia smiled, "You're really okay, for a boy."

Jimmy grinned back. "Just send me a postcard with something nutty on it like, 'Girls can, too!'"

Thinking and Writing About the Selection

1. Who was suspicious of what Amelia and the girls were doing?

2. Why did Jimmy take the blame?

3. Why do you think Amelia said "I'm really flying"?

4. Have you ever made anything that you could ride in? Tell about it.

Applying the Key Skill
Follow Directions

Choose and write the directions below which show how Amelia might have built her ride. Then number the directions in the correct order.

1. Amelia put the boards together to make a track.

2. Amelia looked for boards that were all the same size.

3. Amelia looked for an orange crate to use for a car.

4. Amelia used car wheels on the crate.

5. Amelia found an old banana box.

FOLLOW DIRECTIONS

People who fly airplanes and rockets have to follow a long list of directions. Just to get an airplane off the ground takes many steps. Sometimes the people in a rocket get their directions from helpers on the ground.

ACTIVITY A Read the story. Then follow the directions.

Ann flew into space in a rocket ship. She could see the planet Mars. It looked red. She flew past three asteroids. Two comets zoomed past her. Then she found the satellite she was looking for. She parked her rocket ship. Then she fixed the broken satellite.

1. Write a list of everything Ann saw in space. Be sure to show how many of each thing.
2. Add up all the things on your list.

224

ACTIVITY B Look at this chart of the planets that go around the sun. After you have read the questions, follow the directions below.

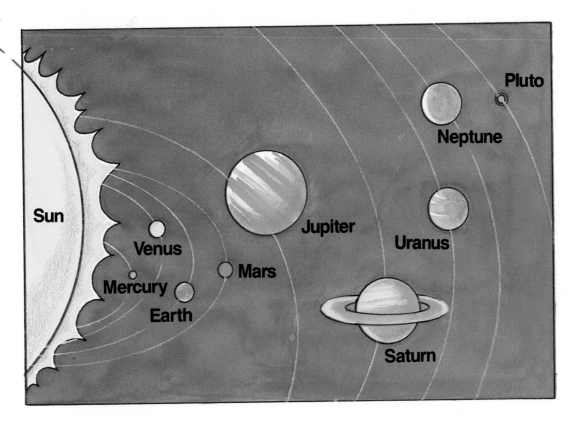

Which planet is called the red planet?
Which planet is between Saturn and Neptune?
Which planet do we live on?
Which planet is the biggest?
Which planet is very close to the sun?

1. Answer the questions on your paper.
2. Draw a picture of one of the planets. Then draw yourself in a rocket ship riding by the planet.

ANOTHER WAY TO FLY

Virginia Arnold

Before the age of satellites, space shuttles, or even airplanes, people wanted to fly. Over 200 years ago, people began using large balloons for flying. The prospect of flight seemed both exciting and dangerous to these daring voyagers.

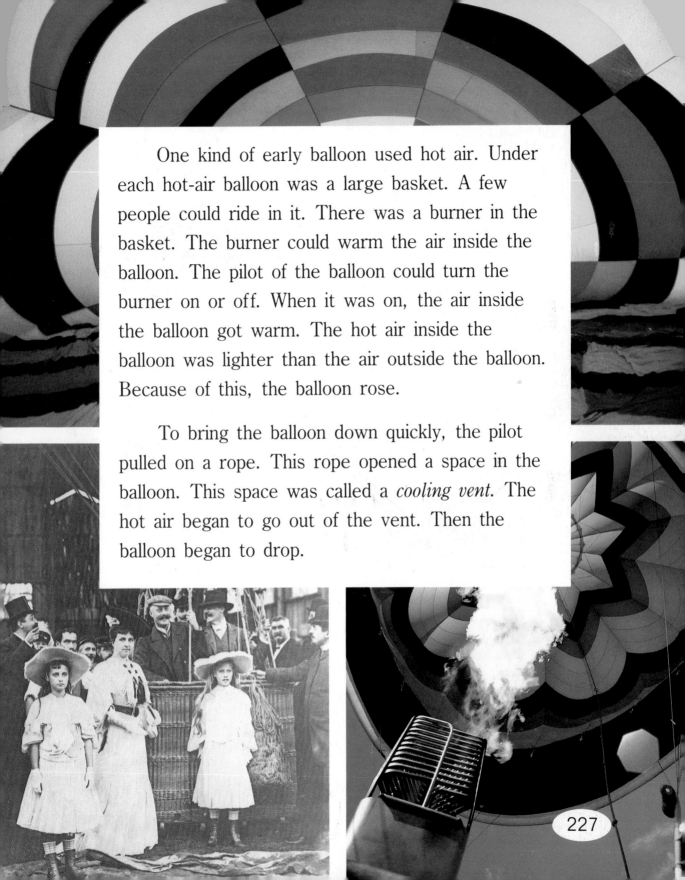

One kind of early balloon used hot air. Under each hot-air balloon was a large basket. A few people could ride in it. There was a burner in the basket. The burner could warm the air inside the balloon. The pilot of the balloon could turn the burner on or off. When it was on, the air inside the balloon got warm. The hot air inside the balloon was lighter than the air outside the balloon. Because of this, the balloon rose.

To bring the balloon down quickly, the pilot pulled on a rope. This rope opened a space in the balloon. This space was called a *cooling vent*. The hot air began to go out of the vent. Then the balloon began to drop.

Another kind of early flying balloon used gas. The gas inside the balloon was lighter than the air outside the balloon. Because of this, the balloon rose. The pilot carried sandbags in the basket. The pilot would throw out a few sandbags. Then the balloon was light enough to rise.

To bring the gas balloon down, the pilot threw out a heavy rope. This rope was called a *dragline*. As the balloon came down, a person on the ground would grab the dragline. This would slow the balloon down.

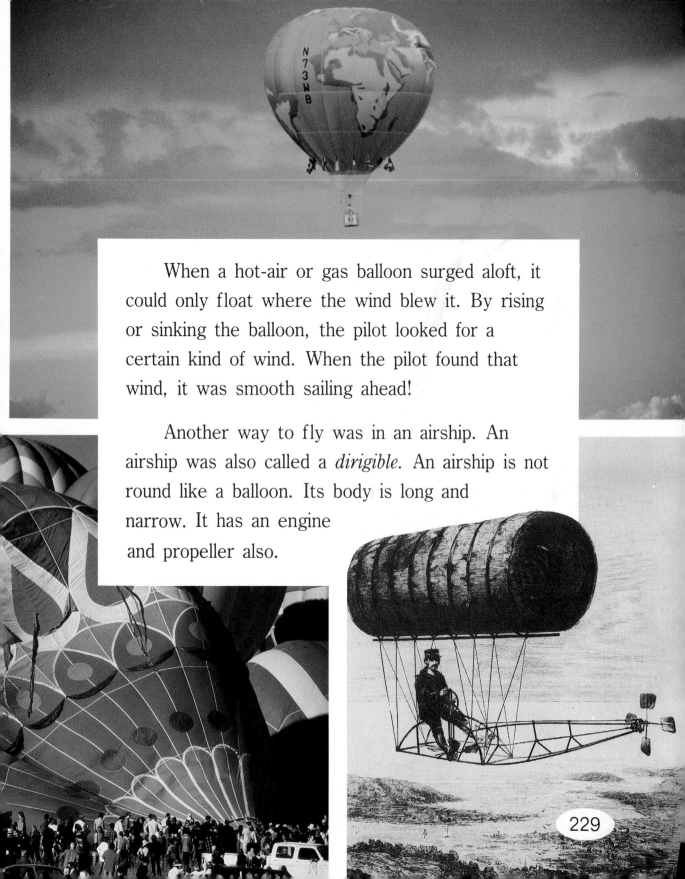

When a hot-air or gas balloon surged aloft, it could only float where the wind blew it. By rising or sinking the balloon, the pilot looked for a certain kind of wind. When the pilot found that wind, it was smooth sailing ahead!

Another way to fly was in an airship. An airship was also called a *dirigible*. An airship is not round like a balloon. Its body is long and narrow. It has an engine and propeller also.

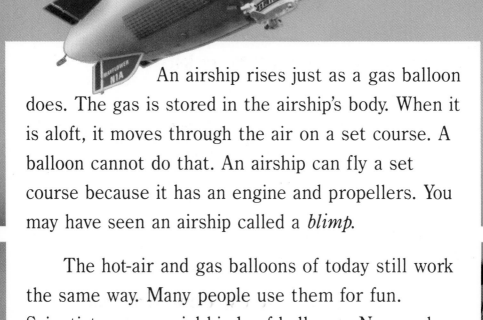

An airship rises just as a gas balloon does. The gas is stored in the airship's body. When it is aloft, it moves through the air on a set course. A balloon cannot do that. An airship can fly a set course because it has an engine and propellers. You may have seen an airship called a *blimp*.

The hot-air and gas balloons of today still work the same way. Many people use them for fun. Scientists use special kinds of balloons. No people fly in them. These balloons help us learn about weather, the stars, and the planets.

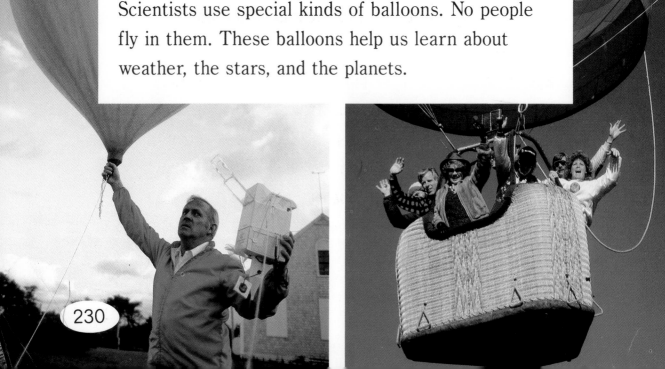

Thinking and Writing About the Selection

1. What are two ways to fly other than in an airplane?

2. How did the pilot of a gas balloon get off the ground?

3. Why do you think people of long ago wanted to fly?

 4. Would you like to fly in a balloon or an airship? Write about an imaginary adventure.

Applying the Key Skill
Alphabetize Words

Read each column of words below. Write each column in the correct alphabetical order on your paper.

age	pool	same
act	prank	sum
about	plus	strip
after	pier	scrap
airplane	photo	smart

231

THE FIRST ZEPPELIN

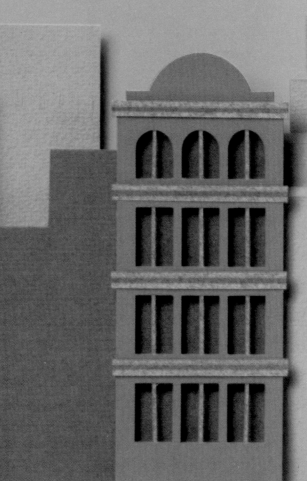

Over the city,
Great ship of grey,
Out of the East you came
One golden day.

Silvered by sunlight,
Nosing along,
Humming contentedly
Your sailing song.

"Someday you'll travel,"
Grandmother said,
"In a long silver ship
High over head."

James S. Tippett

HOT-AIR HENRY

Mary Calhoun

You have been reading about how people wanted to learn to fly. Do you think an animal might like to fly, too? This is a story about Henry, a wise cat who wants to fly in a hot-air balloon. The Man always says, "I'm not flying with that cat!" One day when the balloon is ready to go, Henry sees his chance to stow away. Can Henry fly the balloon?

Henry raced across the snow and leaped up to the basket. One of his claws caught on the cord that fired the burner. There was a horrible roar.

"Grab that cat!" yelled The Man. The Kid grabbed for Henry and slipped on the snow. The burner kept roaring. Flames heated the air. Up rose the balloon. Up rose Henry, up, up, and away! Henry was flying!

He shook his claw loose from the cord. The burner stopped roaring, but the balloon kept on lifting. Henry crouched on the edge of the basket, digging in his claws. Below, the ground fell away. The people shouted and waved. Yet the basket didn't feel as if it were moving, and Henry wasn't afraid.

"Yow-meow!" he called down to The Kid. He was Hot-Air Henry, the flying cat!

The balloon surged up the sky. Looking
down, Henry saw the river like a black ribbon
winding between white fields. The Kid and
The Man looked small as cats. Henry loved the
glorious bubble that carried him across the sky.

But now he'd had his flight. It was The
Man's turn to solo. Time to go down. How?
Henry stood up and tried pulling the cord.
The roar of the burner scared him, and he
tottered on the edge of the basket. To keep
from falling, he clung to the cord, and the
burner kept roaring. The balloon rose higher.
That was not the way to get down out of
the sky.

Henry hopped to the basket floor. He
looked for something to push or pull that
meant *Down*. Nothing. Standing on his hind
legs, he looked over the edge of the basket.
He couldn't see his people anymore. And the
balloon was sailing toward the mountains.

Henry glared up into the bright cave of
the balloon. "Come on down now!" he
yowled. Then he saw a cord leading down
from the balloon. He could reach it from the
edge of the basket. When he clawed the cord,
he saw a little hole of sky open in the balloon
cloth. As air spilled out, the balloon began
to sink.

Faster and faster, the basket dropped
toward the ground—too fast! Henry let go of
the cord. More slowly the basket sank toward
the river, black rushing water—a splash down?

No, the basket crunched on the snowy
bank. "Ha!" breathed Henry. But the basket
bounced up in the air again! Touch and
bounce over the snow. "Stop it!" Henry yelled
at the balloon. "I'm not a yo-yo!"

Ahead were some trees dotted with
blackbirds singing, "O-kal-lee!" The basket
sailed over the tops of the trees, brushing out
birds. The birds flew around the basket. Henry
grabbed at this bird, that bird. Missed! Missed!

The birds flew upward, teasing,
"O-kal-lee, you can't catch me!"

Henry forgot about landing. "I can, too!"
he yowled. Standing on the edge, he pulled
the burner cord. *Roar*, the basket zoomed after
the birds. "Yow-meow!" Henry chased
blackbirds up the sky.

But the balloon overshot the birds, and
they flew back down in the trees. The balloon
sailed on toward the mountains. The wrong
way, away from The Man and The Kid.

"Go back!" yowled Henry at the beautiful
bubble. But the balloon went where the wind
took it.

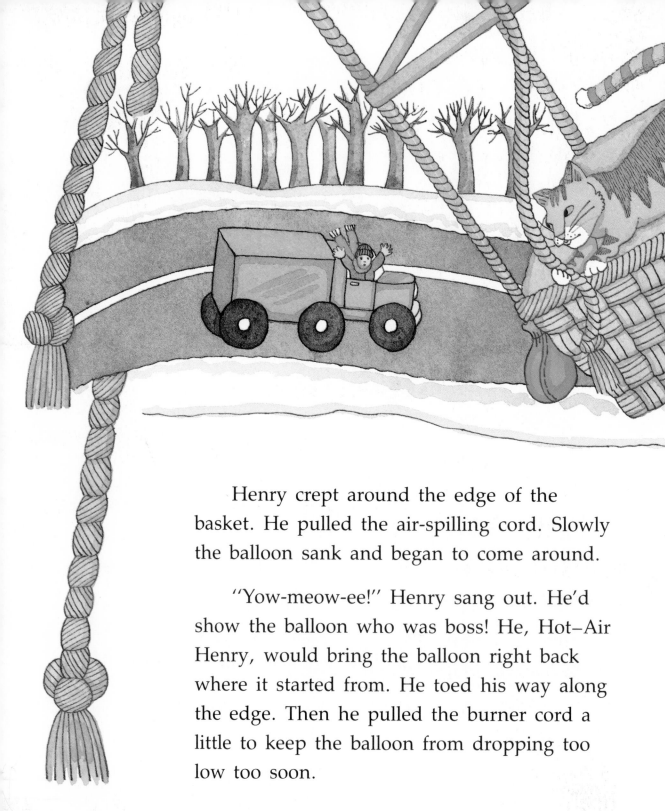

Henry crept around the edge of the
basket. He pulled the air-spilling cord. Slowly
the balloon sank and began to come around.

"Yow-meow-ee!" Henry sang out. He'd
show the balloon who was boss! He, Hot–Air
Henry, would bring the balloon right back
where it started from. He toed his way along
the edge. Then he pulled the burner cord a
little to keep the balloon from dropping too
low too soon.

Henry looked down. Below on a road was
a truck. The Kid's head stuck out the window.
The chase truck was following the balloon.
"Yow-yow, right now!" sang Henry.

Just then, "Honk, honk," came a V of
geese flying straight at him. "Honk!" called
the geese.

"What did they mean, *honk*?" He would
not get out of the way!

The V of geese broke up around the
balloon. They rushed up and down, honking.
But the head goose sat down on the edge of
the basket by the burner cord. "Snaaa!" hissed
Henry. "Get out of my basket! You can't
sit there!"

"Honk! I can, too," said the head goose,
sitting there. The balloon kept sinking.

"Hey cat!" The Kid's shout made Henry
look. The basket was headed for some power
lines. He had to fire the burner to lift quickly,
or he'd cook on the wires. But the goose
guarded the burner cord.

Henry started toward the goose, "Snaaa!"

"Hiss!" answered the goose.

Henry had never fought a goose. He didn't like to try for the first time while balancing like a tightrope walker. But he had to fire the burner! Henry leaped. Over the goose's head he leaped, onto the goose's back. He clawed at the cord. As Henry flew over, a sharp nip of a beak on his tail made him yowl.

But when the burner boomed, the goose jumped into the air. And Henry fell off its back—into the basket, which soared up over the power lines.

Henry licked his throbbing tail, and the geese flew on. "Honk, honk."

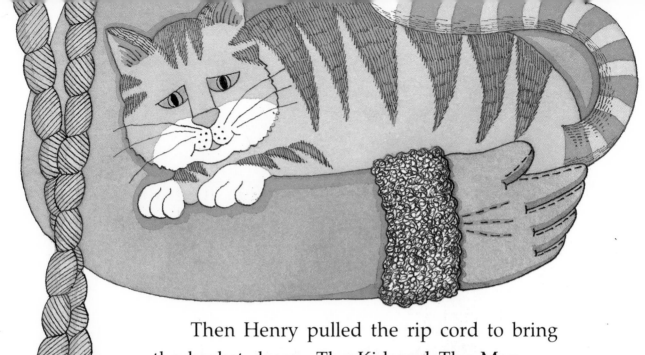

Then Henry pulled the rip cord to bring the basket down. The Kid and The Man jumped out of the truck. The basket bounced once over the snow toward them. Henry hung on to the air-spilling cord. The Man grabbed the dragline, then the basket.

"Mew." The Man might be mad at him for going off with the balloon. Henry leaned his head on The Man's chest. "Purr-mew!" he begged pardon for soloing sooner than The Man.

"Wow, some high-flying cat!" said The Kid, punching down balloon cloth.

"Purr-mew!" said Henry, smoothing The Man's chest. Wise old flying cat.

Thinking and Writing About the Selection

1. How did Henry get into the hot-air balloon?

2. Why wasn't Henry able to get down when he pulled the cord?

3. Why do you think Henry forgot about landing the balloon when he saw the blackbirds?

4. Would you like to go up in a hot-air balloon like Henry? Why or why not?

Applying the Key Skill
Initial Consonant Clusters

Use the letters below to finish the words. Write the words on your paper.

scr   spr   squ   str   thr   tw

In the ___ing, Henry wanted to fly. Once, he was almost ___own out of a balloon. He saw a ___in engine airplane in a field. Henry ___uggled to get the airplane started. The engine ___eamed when he started it. The wheels made a ___eaking sound.

THE BIG
BALLOON
RACE

Eleanor Coerr
Illustrated by Carolyn Croll

Ariel wanted to be an aeronaut and fly in a big balloon like her mother, Carlotta the Great.

"When you are older," said her mother and father.

Carlotta was going to fly her balloon, *Lucky Star*, in a race against Bernard the Brave and his balloon, *Flying Cloud*. On the day of the big race, Ariel fell asleep inside the basket. Her mother didn't see her until it was too late. She was flying after all!

With a jolt, *Lucky Star* took off. Ariel woke up. "What happened?" she asked.

Carlotta stared. "Ariel! What have you done?" she cried. "We are aloft!"

Ariel looked over the side. Sure enough, they were off the ground. Below, someone yelled, "Stop! There is a stowaway in that basket!" Ariel's father waved his arms and shouted something.

Ariel waved back. "Oooo!" she cried. "It's like being a bird." She watched the people set out for the finish line. Some were in buggies. Some were in wagons. Others were on fast horses.

A crosswind tugged at the balloon. WHOOOSH! *Lucky Star* dived down over a farm. Dogs barked and ran around in circles. Pigs squealed. Chickens squawked. A horse reared and galloped away.

SCRUUUNCH! *Lucky Star*'s basket scraped the tops of the trees.

"Can we go higher?" asked Ariel.

"The balloon and ballast are for only one passenger," said Carlotta. "You are extra weight." She dropped one bag of sand over the side. Up went *Lucky Star*. The farm got smaller and smaller. It looked like a toy. Then it was gone.

"Oh my!" said Carlotta. "An updraft is carrying us into that raincloud." She pulled on the blue valve rope to let out some gas. *Lucky Star* did not fall.

Ariel stared up at the balloon. "Why don't you pull the red rope, too?" she asked.

"That is the rip cord," said her mother. "It lets the gas out all at once." Carlotta tied her hat under her chin. "Sit down!" she ordered. "And hang on!" *Lucky Star* was in the middle of a wet, bumpy cloud. The basket went back and forth, up and down, then around and around.

"I feel sick," said Ariel.

"A good aeronaut keeps calm," said
Carlotta. "The balloon will cool. Then we will
go down." She was right. In a few minutes
Lucky Star was sailing away from the cloud.

Carlotta checked everything. "Ropes and toggles are in fine trim," she said. She read the altimeter that hung around her neck. "We are about 2,000 feet up." She read the map and compass. "We are heading south."

"Look!" said Ariel. "The lake is straight ahead."

"The finish line is on the other side of the lake," said Carlotta.

Just then they saw *Flying Cloud*. "He is beating us," said Ariel. "He will win the gold medal."

Carlotta shook her head. "I have a few tricks yet," she said. "Maybe we can find a faster stream of air below us." She let some gas out of the balloon. Down . . . down . . . down went *Lucky Star*. It was sinking too fast—and toward a town! Carlotta tossed handfuls of sand over the side. *Lucky Star* moved up and skimmed over the houses. People stopped whatever they were doing and stared at the balloon.

Suddenly wind bit Ariel's cheeks.

"Heigh-ho!" cried Carlotta. "We found the airstream!"

It was Ariel who first saw a church steeple coming toward them. "Look out!" she yelled. She closed her eyes and hung on. Carlotta threw out more sand. Just in time! *Lucky Star* soared over the steeple. Now *Flying Cloud* was behind.

"If we don't hit another updraft," said Carlotta, "we might win." Soon they were flying over the lake. "There is only a little sand left," Carlotta said. "Let's hope the wind blows us right across." The air was cold. *Lucky Star*'s gas cooled. They went down. Carlotta tossed out the last handful of sand. But it was not enough.

"Oh," cried Ariel. "We'll crash into the lake!"

"Let's make the basket lighter," said Carlotta. Ariel helped throw out everything they didn't need. *Lucky Star* wobbled! It took a giant step.

"Lean on this side," said Carlotta. The basket creaked and leaned toward shore. *Lucky Star* was almost there, when SPLAAAAASH! The basket plunked into the water. But it didn't sink. The balloon kept it afloat.

"We lost the race," cried Ariel, "and it is all my fault. I am extra weight." Ariel knew what she had to do. She held her nose and jumped into the lake. The water was only up to her waist.

"Goodness me!" said her mother. "That was brave, but it will not help. Even without you, the basket is too wet and heavy to go up again."

Just then *Flying Cloud* began to come down.
"Our last chance!" cried Carlotta. She threw a
rope to Ariel. "Pull! Pull us to land! Hurry!"

Ariel grabbed the rope and waded onto
the beach. *Lucky Star* was easy to pull with a
balloon holding it up.

"Splendid!" cried Carlotta. She jumped
out and dragged the basket to higher ground.
A minute later *Flying Cloud* landed.

"We won! We won!" shouted Ariel and
her mother. They were laughing and hugging
and crying all at the same time.

Bernard the Brave tied his balloon
to a tree. Then he came over and shook
hands. "Congratulations!" he said. "I see the
Lucky Star has a crew." He put a blanket
around Ariel.

"Thank you, sir," said Ariel.

Bernard smiled. "Why, it is my pleasure."

Soon the crowd arrived. Ariel's father rode up in the buggy. He heard how Ariel had helped win the race.

"Ariel," he said, "I'm proud of you." The mayor gave Ariel the gold medal.

Carlotta hugged Ariel. "I'm proud of you, too," she said. "Maybe you are old enough to fly."

Ariel smiled happily. She was sure of it.

Thinking and Writing About the Selection

1. What could Ariel see from the balloon?

2. Why did the *Lucky Star* go higher when Carlotta threw sand out of the basket?

3. Why do you think Ariel said being in a balloon is "like being a bird"?

 4. Have you ever been in some kind of a race? Write about it.

Applying the Key Skill
Main Idea

Read the following paragraph about "The Big Balloon Race." Then copy the paragraph and draw a line under the main idea. Draw two lines under the supporting details.

Ariel had always wanted to fly. When she was a baby, she watched her mother go up in a balloon for the first time. When she grew older, she followed her mother each time she went to the balloon. She imagined that she was going up with her.

SKILLS activity

MAIN IDEA

A paragraph is a group of sentences. One sentence usually tells you the main idea of the paragraph. All the other sentences in a paragraph tell details about, or support the main idea. The main idea sentence tells what the paragraph is about.

Read the paragraphs below. Think about the main idea and supporting details. Then read the questions and write the answers on your paper.

ACTIVITY A A hot-air balloon race is a beautiful thing to see. Even if you stay on the ground, you will have fun. Each balloon is different. The balloons have different colors and pictures on them. At first all the balloons are on the ground. Then they fill up with air and take off. When all the balloons are in the sky, it looks like a dream.

1. What is the main idea sentence?
   a. Each balloon is different.
   b. A hot-air balloon race is a beautiful thing to see.

258

2. Which supporting detail tells you what the balloons look like?

    a. Even if you stay on the ground, you will have fun.

    b. The balloons have different colors and pictures on them.

ACTIVITY B People have always wanted to fly like birds. They have made all kinds of machines to fly. Most of the machines never worked. But one very old kind of flying machine that does work is a hot-air balloon. Some people would rather fly in a balloon than in a plane. They think being outside in the air is more like being a bird.

1. What is the main idea sentence?

    a. They have made all kinds of machines to fly.

    b. People have always wanted to fly like birds.

2. Which detail sentence tells you about most flying machines?

    a. Most of the machines never worked.

    b. Some people would rather fly in a balloon than in a plane.

THE KITE-MAKERS

Susan Renner-Smith

In the year 1903, Wilbur and Orville Wright were the first people ever to fly an airplane. How did they come to do such a wondrous thing? From the time that they were boys they thought about flying. This is a story about the Wright brothers as boys, and how they learned something about flying.

260

"Oh no!" shouted Orville Wright. "My kite is sinking."

Wilbur Wright ran to help. He was too late. Crash! The kite smashed against a tree.

Orville looked at the bent sticks and twisted paper. "This cost us thirty-five cents," he said sadly.

Thirty-five cents was a lot of money over 100 years ago, when the Wright brothers were boys. But Wilbur had an idea.

"Come on," Wilbur said. "We can make a better kite."

"You think so?" asked Orville.

"You bet!" said Wilbur. Off the brothers raced for home.

"Mother," Orville called. "We are going to make a kite. It will fly better than any from the store."

His mother gave him a serious look. "How will you make it better?" she asked.

"First, I'll take this one apart. I want to see how it is made," answered Orville. He began to pull the paper off the kite.

"A kite is really a flying machine, isn't it, Mother?" asked Wilbur.

"In a way," she answered. "But what do you think makes it fly?"

Orville looked at the broken kite. "I think the wind pushes on the paper, as it pushes on a sail," he said. "Maybe we should use more paper to catch more wind."

"But birds' wings don't look like sails," said Wilbur. "The wings are round on top like this." He made his hands look like wings. "We should make the cross piece round to look more like wings."

Orville waved the broken kite around. "A kite isn't a bird," he shouted.

"The wind will push a round cross piece higher," said Wilbur.

"It won't," said Orville in a loud voice.

262

"It will," yelled Wilbur. He grabbed a pencil and paper. "I'll show you."

He began to draw a picture of a kite. "Wrong!" said Orville. He made another picture. Soon the boys stopped yelling. They began to draw kites together.

Suddenly, they said, "That's it!" Orville showed their mother. The kite in the picture was extra big. Its cross piece was round on top like the wings of a bird. Numbers were written all over the picture.

"Those numbers tell how long the sticks for the kite should be," Orville told his mother. "These tell the size of the paper. Now we'll MAKE it!"

Together, the two boys ran to the wood shed. They cut sticks. They cut paper. They put on glue. They did each step with care.

Then the Wright brothers took their new kite to the hill. Other children were flying kites there.

"Look at that funny kite," shouted one boy.

"It's too big," said another.

"Don't worry, Orville," said Wilbur. "Let's just show them." He ran into the wind.

The big kite flew straight up into the sky. Higher and higher it rose.

"Come help me, Orville," shouted Wilbur. "I'm going to fly away."

Suddenly, the wind died down. Children groaned. Other kites fell from the sky.

But not the Wright brothers' kite. The extra
paper caught the light wind. It lifted the round
cross piece. The kite flew high until the boys
pulled it down.

"Hey, what do you want for that kite?" called a boy.

"We'll sell it for twenty cents," Orville said.

"Make me one," said a girl.

"I'll buy one, too," said another child.

So Wilbur and Orville made more kites. They tried to make each one fly faster and higher.

When the brothers grew up, they decided to try and make a flying machine. This machine would be large enough for a person. Other people had tried to make such a machine. Most of the machines had crashed to earth.

The Wrights had ideas about how to make a safe flying machine. To try out these ideas, Wilbur built a giant box kite. It worked! Then the Wright brothers put a small engine on that giant kite. In 1903, after many tests, their flying machine rose into the air. The Wright brothers had done it. They had made an airplane!

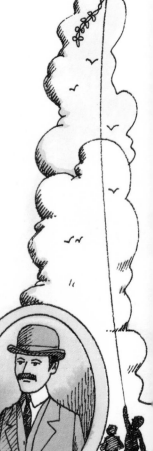

Thinking and Writing About the Selection

1. What did Wilbur and Orville use to make their kite?

2. What did the brothers do *before* they began to build their kite?

3. Why didn't Wilbur and Orville go to the store and buy another kite?

4. If you could invent something, what would it be?

Applying the Key Skill
Short Vowels

Look at the underlined letter in each key word. Then find the word in the row that has the same vowel sound. Write the word on your paper.

1. about   a. answers b. again   c. bat   d. part

2. taken   a. they   b. week   c. person d. then

3. pencil a. like   b. wait   c. children d. tried

4. pilot   a. do   b. boat   c. know   d. second

5. helpful a. travel   b. you   c. ruin   d. could

There Was
A Young Person
Named Bly

There was a young person named Bly
Who ambitiously wanted to fly,
    So he said magic things
      And he grew him some wings,
And now he is going—good-by!

Myra Cohn Livingston

269

SUMI'S PRIZE

Yoshiko Uchida

Making kites helped the Wright brothers learn about flying. Sumi hopes that flying kites will help her in another way.

Just once Sumi wanted to win a prize. She was seven and in the second grade. She tried hard, but she never won anything. Her teacher was the mayor of Sugi Village. Everyone called him Mr. Mayor. He had a shiny black top hat that he wore to all the festivals in the village.

One day Mr. Mayor tells the children about a kite flying contest on New Year's Day. There will be a prize for the best and most beautiful kite. Sumi and her brother, Taro, work hard to make their kites. Finally Sumi's great gold and black butterfly kite is ready. Who will win the contest?

Now that the kite was ready, Sumi
could hardly wait for New Year's Day. She
waited and worried as the first snow came.
But when New Year's Day came at last,
the weather was bright and clear. It
was just right for flying kites.

There were already many people
at the river's edge when Sumi and her
family arrived. Sumi saw the girls in her
class. Not one was holding a kite. Sumi
swallowed hard. She saw that she was the
only girl to enter the contest.

Sumi saw Mr. Mayor in his shiny top hat.
He bowed as he wished everyone a happy
new year.

Now the boys lined up in front of him with
their kites, and Mother wished Sumi good luck.

271

Sumi found a place at the end of the line and looked anxiously at the other kites. There were all kinds of kites of all sizes and shapes. But nobody else had a butterfly. Sumi thought her kite was the most beautiful kite of them all. Mr. Mayor walked up and down looking at the kites. "Very fine," he said, "very fine." He stopped in front of Sumi. "Ah," he said but that was all.

Sumi wanted to tell him how hard she had worked on her kite, but her tongue wouldn't move. She wanted to wish him a happy new year, too. But all she could do was scratch the tip of her nose.

Then it was time to get the kites up.
Father helped Sumi get her butterfly into the
air, and then it was all up to her. Carefully,
carefully, she let out the string, tugging to
keep her butterfly climbing higher and higher.

"Climb! Climb!" Sumi shouted to her
butterfly.

It seemed to hear her, for it soared up
and up, straight toward the sun. From the
corner of her eye, Sumi could see her brother
Taro's kite. It was soaring too, but her
butterfly was going higher. It truly was. Sumi
knew that she would win. If she could beat
Taro, she knew she could beat anyone. Now
at last, she would have her prize!

273

Sumi glanced at Mr. Mayor to be sure
that he saw her kite. He was watching it with
his head tipped back, shading his eyes from
the sun. And then it happened! A gust of
wind swooped along the bank of the river
and swept his top hat right off his head. It
went whirling along the sand straight toward
the water.

"My hat!" Mr. Mayor shouted. "My hat!"

"Stop," Sumi shouted. "Mr. Mayor's hat!"
But everyone was too busy looking up to see
what was going on below.

It was hard to watch her kite and the hat as well, but Sumi knew she must help Mr. Mayor. Now the hat was at the water's edge and Sumi had to save it. She took one last look at her beautiful butterfly. Then, holding tight to its string, she ran as fast as she could.

She threw herself on the hat with a great thud and felt it flatten below her. She had saved the hat, but she had squashed it flat. Worse still, she had given her kite such a jerk, it turned upside down and came tumbling from the sky. Her beautiful butterfly soared to earth and fell in a heap on the sand.

"Ohhhh." A sad cry went through the crowd, for now everyone saw what had happened.

Mr. Mayor ran to Sumi's side. "Are you all right, little one?" he asked. He helped her to her feet.

Sumi nodded, but she could not keep back her tears.

"My kite's broken," she said sadly. "And I squashed your hat."

Mr. Mayor looked sad, too. "I am sorry about your kite," he said. "It was a fine kite, but don't worry about my hat. Watch," he said, and he whacked the hat on his arm. It popped right up. "Come with me," he said, and he led her to the judging table.

Mother and Father rushed to Sumi's side. "Are you all right?" they asked. "We saw you save Mr. Mayor's hat," they added proudly.

The mayor let Sumi sit beside him at the judging table. And they watched the bright kites in the sky together.

276

Sumi saw Taro's kite soaring above all the others and she knew he would win. Now he would have the prize while she still had none. Sumi wanted to cry. She had come so close to winning.

Soon it was time to pull down the kites. The prize was a beautiful box of water-color paints. Everyone clapped when it went to Taro, for his kite had truly flown best of all. The contest was over, and people began to walk away.

Mr. Mayor, however, was not finished. "Just a minute," he said. He fumbled about in his pockets. Finally he pulled out his big blue fountain pen.

"I seem to have another prize," he said. "It is for the only girl to enter the contest and the only person in Sugi Village to save a top hat from the river!"

Then the mayor shook Sumi's hand and gave her his own fountain pen. Sumi was sure she must be dreaming. Everyone clapped and cheered.

"The mayor's own pen," they said in excited voices. "That's the best prize there ever was."

Sumi could not find words for the big happiness inside her. Suddenly, Sumi knew that she no longer needed to worry about winning anything. Today she had done something nobody else in Sugi Village could ever do again. In fact, who in all of Japan could enter a kite contest and win the mayor's own fountain pen for saving his hat? Nobody, Sumi thought happily, nobody but me!

Thinking and Writing About the Selection

1. When was the kite flying contest held?

2. Why didn't Sumi win the contest?

3. How do you think Sumi made a kite that looked like a butterfly?

4. Have you ever tried very hard to win something? Tell about it.

Applying the Key Skill
Draw Conclusions

Use complete sentences to answer the following questions about "Sumi's Prize."

1. Why did Sumi want to win the kite flying contest so badly?

2. Why do you think Sumi saved the mayor's hat?

3. Why do you know that Sumi is proud of herself when the contest is over?

Commander Toad and the Planet of the Grapes

Jane Yolen

Illustrated by Bruce Degen

There are many ships that fly from star to star. But only one is long and green. Only one is flown by Commander Toad.

Brave and bright, bright and brave, Commander Toad brings his ship through deep hopper space. That ship is called the Star Warts. Its mission: to find new worlds, to explore new planets, to bring a little bit of Earth out to the alien stars.

Commander Toad has a very fine crew. Mr. Hop is his copilot who thinks a lot. Lieutenant Lily is in charge of the engine room. Young Jake Skyjumper makes the maps and old Doc Peeper, in his grass-green wig, keeps them healthy.

Many days and many nights go by in space.

At last a new planet comes into sight. "It is a fine place for my tired crew," says brave and bright Commander Toad. The *Star Warts* hangs over the planet like a great green pickle.

Commander Toad and Lieutenant Lily sail down in a little sky skimmer. They will make sure that nothing nasty or mean waits for the crew on this brand-new world.

Commander Toad leaps out of the skimmer and laughs as he lands. "A fine, quiet planet for a picnic. Come join me, Lieutenant Lily."

Lily smiles. Then she sneezes. *"Ah-chippity-choo.* There is something on this calm world I am allergic to," she says and sneezes once again. She wipes her nose with a regulation starfleet nose-kerchief and prepares to leap from the skimmer. But before she can move, something begins to grow under Commander Toad's feet.

First it is a bump. Then it is a lump. Then it is a bubble that looks like a giant grape. "Wait a bit," warns Commander Toad. "Things grow too quickly on this quiet world."

The bump-lump-grape has become a bunch of twenty or more bumpy-lumpy things. They move like player-piano keys under Commander Toad, playing a silly tickle song on the bottoms of his webbed feet. "Ho-ho-ho," sings Commander Toad. Hop-hop-hop go his feet.

"Quick, Commander," Lieutenant Lily calls, sneezing twice. She leans over the skimmer's side, holding one hand to her nose and the other hand out to Commander Toad. "Stop hopping around and hop in." But it is too late. As she watches, one lump-bump grows up and around Commander Toad and swallows him.

"*Burp!*" says the bubble grape.

"Oh, Commander," Lieutenant Lily cries.

She will go back up to the *Star Warts*. She will ask the others to help. Mr. Hop will think. Old Doc Peeper will bring Band-Aids. And young Jake Skyjumper will stay on the ship. "Don't go away, Commander Toad," says Lieutenant Lily, "*Ah-chippity-choo.*"

284

"*Burp!*" says the grape. Commander Toad says nothing. Lieutenant Lily pushes the button that sends the skimmer up to the waiting ship.

On board again, Lily tells them all what has happened.

Mr. Hop thinks for a moment, his chin in his hand. "Very interesting," says old Doc Peeper. "I'll get my bag."

Then Doc Peeper and Lieutenant Lily and Mr. Hop ride the skimmer down. Only young Jake is left aboard to guide the great ship home if anything bad happens to the rest of the crew on the calm but scary Planet of the Grapes. The skimmer hovers above the planet, where only a bunch of great grapes waits to greet them. "One of those grapes is Commander Toad, brave and bright, bright and brave," says Lieutenant Lily. She sneezes.

"Which one?" asks Mr. Hop.

"I do not know," says Lieutenant Lily. "All grapes look alike to me."

"That one might be the commander," says Mr. Hop. "The one with the lump where his hat would be." Mr. Hop calls down to the lumpy grape. "Don't worry, Commander. We are here to help." He turns to the others. "I have been thinking: As long as we move very fast, there will be no time for a grape to grab us." He hops out.

286

"Wait!" cries Lily, ending with a sneeze. But it is too late. No sooner do Mr. Hop's feet touch the ground than a bunch of grapes grows like blisters all around him. One grape, bigger than the rest, swallows Mr. Hop.

"*Burp!*" says the grape.

"*Ah-chippity-choo*," says Lieutenant Lily sadly.

"Very interesting," says old Doc Peeper. He fixes his wig. Then he takes a great big needle out of his bag. "Before we save Commander Toad and Mr. Hop from being graped, I will give you a shot to stop your sneezes and your *chippity-choos*. It is hard to be brave when your nose is running faster than your feet."

But while Doc Peeper moves toward Lieutenant Lily's side of the skimmer, an enormous bubble is growing underneath them. It grows up and around the skimmer, quiet as air, silent as sleep. And before Lieutenant Lily can sneeze or old Doc Peeper can give her a shot, the skimmer is caught in the biggest lump of them all.

"This bump is so big, it must be Alexander the grape," says Lieutenant Lily.

Doc Peeper groans. It is dark inside the grape, and hot. Doc Peeper finds his flashlight. He turns it on. It makes things brighter but it does not make them clearer.

Suddenly the sky skimmer tips sideways, and head over heels, webbed feet over wig, Lieutenant Lily and Doc Peeper are spilled out. Lieutenant Lily falls on her gun and it jams. Doc Peeper falls on the handle of his needle. The needle goes into the bubble—*Whoosh!*—and most of the medicine is shot into the bubble's side.

"*Burp!*" says Alexander the grape.

289

"Ah-chippity-choo," Lieutenant Lily replies. Then far above them is a sudden pinprick of light. Is it a window? Is it a star? Is it an opening in the top of the grape? Doc Peeper gives Lily the rest of the medicine and then he gives her a boost up. She sticks her head out of the hole and looks around. The opening grows wider. Lieutenant Lily crawls through.

Soon the grape has opened like a flower. Doc Peeper steps out. "I do not get it," says Lieutenant Lily.

Doc Peeper says, "I do." He takes another needle out of his black bag and goes over to the lump with the hat.

No sooner does he give the lump a shot than the grape peels itself and out steps Commander Toad. "Have a grape day," says Commander Toad, shaking Doc Peeper's hand.

Doc Peeper gives a final shot to the Mr. Hop lump. When Mr. Hop steps out, he looks around. "I am very grapeful to be out of there," he says.

Commander Toad leaps into the skimmer, and behind him come Mr. Hop, Lieutenant Lily, and old Doc Peeper. The sky skimmer lifts off. "What was that all about?" asks Commander Toad.

Doc Peeper smiles. "Just as Lily is allergic to the planet, so this planet is allergic to us. We gave it warts and hives and a bad case of the grapes."

Lieutenant Lily puts her hand to her nose. "No more sneezes," she says. "Your shot worked on me."

They look over the side of the skimmer. Far below, on the planet, they can see only one grape left. It is wearing a silly green wig. "And it worked on the planet, too," says Lieutenant Lily.

"Hummmmmm," says Mr. Hop. "If the planet is allergic to us, it would not be a good idea to go back again. Besides, those grapes were an awfully tight fit."

"And they liked to *wine* a lot," says Commander Toad. He slaps his leg and laughs at his own joke.

Old Doc Peeper looks serious. "There is something more," he says as he puts the needle into the bag. "Anyone who sets foot on that planet seems to tell very bad grape jokes."

293

"Bad?" says Commander Toad. "I thought those jokes were the grapest."

The sky skimmer floats up to the mother ship. Jake Skyjumper welcomes them aboard. "I think we got away just in time," says Commander Toad. "There is *nothing* worse than a *bad* grape joke."

"I do not get it," says Jake Skyjumper.

"Just be glad that they did not get you," says Lieutenant Lily.

They tell him all about it as the ship takes off into deep hopper space. "Let's find some new planets," says Commander Toad. Then they leapfrog across the galaxy from star to star to star.

Soaring

You read about many kinds of flight in *Soaring*. Some of the stories told about flying in imaginary spaceships while others told about soaring away in balloons. Think about your favorite way to soar up and away!

Thinking and Writing About *Soaring*

1. Who made their own flying machines?

2. Why is the sky important in "Spider in the Sky" and "The Big Balloon Race"?

3. How were Harriet's flight and Commander Toad's flight alike?

4. Why do you think Ziggie and Ruthie in "Regards to the Man in the Moon" finally had a good time flying in *IMAGINATION I?*

 5. Use your imagination to think of a *different* way to soar. Write about how you would fly.

This glossary can help you find out the meaning of words in this book that you may not know.

The words are listed in alphabetical order. Guide words at the top of each page tell you the first and last word on the page. Each word is divided into syllables.

The definitions are adapted from the Macmillan *Beginning Dictionary*.

A

a•ble Having the power or skill to do something. "If I stand on the chair, I will be <u>able</u> to get the book," said Jack.

a•board In, on, or into a ship, train, airplane, or other vehicle. Louie helped Susie climb <u>aboard</u> the spaceship.

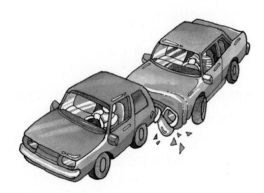

ac•ci•dent Something that happens for no apparent reason and is not expected. The <u>accident</u> happened when Sue fell on the ice.

ad•ven•tures Things a person does that involve danger and difficulties. Mr. Pompey has been around the world on a boat and had many <u>adventures</u>.

ad•vice An idea that is offered to a person telling him or her how to act in a certain situation. Mother gave Nan <u>advice</u> on how to care for the new kitten.

aer•o•naut A pilot of a lighter-than-air craft. Ariel wanted to be an <u>aeronaut</u> and fly in a dirigible.

a•gainst In opposition to; in the opposite direction to; in contact with; so as to strike or come into contact with. Ted was <u>against</u> the idea of having a school bake sale.

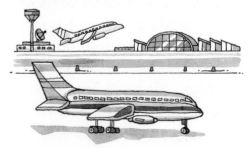

air•port A place with fields for the airplanes to land and take off. We waited at the <u>airport</u> until Mother's plane took off.

al•read•y Before or by this time; previously. I had <u>already</u> started home when I heard my mother calling.

298

al•tim•e•ter An instrument for measuring altitude above sea level or ground. The <u>altimeter</u> showed that the plane was up 20,000 feet.

a•mong In the midst of; surrounded by. There was a package for Jim <u>among</u> the parcels.

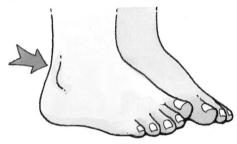

an•kles The joints that connect the feet to the legs. Kim walked out into the lake until the water came up over her <u>ankles</u>.

anx•ious•ly In a nervous or worried way; wanting something eagerly. Beth waited <u>anxiously</u> for the name of the contest winner.

an•y•bod•y Any person whatever; anyone. Does <u>anybody</u> here have the time?

A•sia The largest continent. Can you name one country in <u>Asia</u>?

as•ter•oids The thousands of small, rocky bodies that revolve around the sun. Most of the <u>asteroids</u> are found between the planets Mars and Jupiter.

aw•ful Causing fear, dread, or awe; terrible; very bad. The branch made an <u>awful</u> cracking sound as it fell from the tree.

B

bal•ance A steady position. The woman could keep her <u>balance</u> while walking on a rope high above the ground.

bald Having little or no hair on the head. When the man took off his hat, we saw that he was <u>bald</u>.

299

bal·last Something heavy used to give balance. The hot-air balloon used sandbags as <u>ballast</u>.

bal·loon A bag filled with air or other gas. The large <u>balloon</u> with its basket of passengers floated up into the air.

band·age A strip of cloth or other material used to cover or bind a wound or injury. When Rico cut his hand, Mother put a <u>bandage</u> on it.

bas·kets Goals scored by tossing the ball through the basket in the game of basketball. Jenny made three <u>baskets</u> for our team.

black-stock·inged Wearing or having black stockings. Through the low window, I saw a pair of <u>black-stockinged</u> legs.

blan·ket A covering made of wool, nylon, or other material. It was so cold that Mother put another <u>blanket</u> on Luz's bed.

blimp A small nonrigid airship, used chiefly for observation. The scientists used a <u>blimp</u> to find out about the weather.

blind·ing Taking away the power of sight from; making sightless. The man turned his head away from the <u>blinding</u> light.

blinked Flashed on and off; closed and opened the eyes quickly. The street light <u>blinked</u> off and on.

blue·ber·ry A small, dark-blue, sweet berry with tiny seeds. Freddy ate one <u>blueberry</u> for every two he picked.

300

bod•y The main portion of a human being or animal without the head and limbs; trunk; the whole physical structure and material of a human being, plant, or animal. The <u>body</u> of a bear is covered with fur.

bor•ing Uninteresting and dull. Mark found it <u>boring</u> to wait for the plane.

bot•tom The lowest part; the under or lower part. There is a lake at the <u>bottom</u> of the hill.

Brem•en A port city in northern West Germany. The boat will sail from <u>Bremen</u> for America.

bright•ly In a lively way; cheerfully. Jenny smiled <u>brightly</u> and said, "Good morning!"

broom A brush with a long handle used for sweeping. Jill used a <u>broom</u> to clean the floor of her room.

brought Carried or caused (someone or something) to come with oneself. The man <u>brought</u> a package to our house.

bug•gly Of the nature of or like a bug. The robot had <u>buggly</u> eyes that stuck out from its head.

bug•gy A light carriage with four wheels. The family rode in the <u>buggy</u> pulled by the horse.

build•ing Making by putting parts or material together. Cindy and her father are <u>building</u> a birdhouse.

built See **building.** The children <u>built</u> a special toy and won first prize.

burn•er The part of a stove or furnace from which the flame comes. Father lit the <u>burner</u> to warm the house.

bush•es Woody plants; shrubs. The rabbit hid in the <u>bushes</u>.

bus•y Full of activity; doing something; in use. Carmela was <u>busy</u> all day fixing her toy airplane.

but•ter•flies Insects with a thin body and four large brightly colored wings. There are always many <u>butterflies</u> in the flower bed.

C

calm Not moving; still. The sun was shining, the wind was <u>calm</u>—it was a beautiful day.

can•dles Sticks of wax or tallow formed around a wick, or string, that will burn. My sister will light the <u>candles</u> on my birthday cake.

cap•ture To catch and hold a person, animal, or thing. Have you ever played the game "Capture The Flag"?

care•ful Paying close attention; watchful. Are you always <u>careful</u> when you cross the street?

catch To take or get hold of something or someone that is moving. Mimi can <u>catch</u> the ball as it flies through the air.

caught As in the phrase **caught on:** Became fashionable or popular. The new game <u>caught</u> on, and soon people all across the country were playing it.

cau·tious·ly Carefully. Mr. Raymond moved <u>cautiously</u> through the dark room.

cel·e·brate To observe or honor a special day or event with ceremonies and other activities. We will <u>celebrate</u> Oliver's birthday with a party in the park.

ce·ment A powdery mixture made of limestone and clay. It is mixed with water to form a paste that becomes hard as rock when it dries. Our sidewalk is made of <u>cement</u>.

cen·ti·me·ters Units of length in the metric system. A centimeter is equal to one-hundredth of a meter, or .39 of an inch. Do you know how tall you are in <u>centimeters</u>?

chance A good or favorable opportunity. Would you like to have the <u>chance</u> to go to the Olympic Games?

cheered Gave a shout of praise, happiness, or encouragement; made or became happy. The crowd <u>cheered</u> as the hot-air balloon floated aloft.

Chi·ca·go The largest city in the state of Illinois, on Lake Michigan. Ben and his family will take a trip to <u>Chicago</u> this summer.

Chi·na A country in eastern Asia. There are more people in <u>China</u> than any other country in the world.

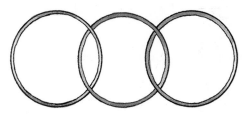

cir·cles Closed curved lines; things that are shaped like circles. The children joined hands and formed two <u>circles</u>, one inside the other.

clay A fine-grained earth that can be molded when wet, but that hardens when dried or baked. Mona made a cup out of <u>clay</u>.

clear Free from anything that darkens; bright; easily seen through; easily seen, heard, or understood. The family chose a lovely, <u>clear</u> day for their picnic.

climbed Moved or went upward. We climbed the hill to the very top.

clos•et A small room for storing things. Carlos put his coat and his skates in his closet.

clump A group or bunch. We decided to have our picnic in a clump of trees by the pond.

com•et A bright heavenly body. A comet travels around the sun and may sometimes come close to earth.

com•pass An instrument for showing directions. Carlos used the compass to find out what direction south was.

con•grat•u•la•tions Good wishes or praise given for a person's success or for something nice that has happened. All of Mimi's friends gave her their congratulations when she won the race.

con•test Something that tests or proves a person's skill or ability, such as a game or race. The school held an art contest for everyone in the school.

con•trap•tion Mechanical device; contrivance; gadget. Everyone wanted to know what the contraption I was building was for.

cook To make food ready for eating by using heat. Uncle Jacob's favorite food to cook is chicken.

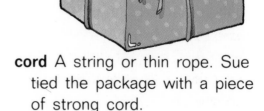

cord A string or thin rope. Sue tied the package with a piece of strong cord.

coun•try Any area of land; region; an area of land that has boundaries and has a government that is shared by all the people; nation. Do you know the name of our country?

course In the phrase **of course:** certainly; naturally. Of <u>course</u> I will come to your party!

cou•sin The son or daughter of an aunt or uncle. My brother, my sister, my <u>cousin</u>, and I will visit our grandmother.

coy•o•te An animal that looks like a wolf and lives in the prairies of North America. A <u>coyote</u> will hunt large animals to eat.

crea•ture A living person or animal. The <u>creature</u> was like no other Sam had ever seen before.

crept Moved slowly and quietly; crawled. The mouse <u>crept</u> out of its hole and looked carefully around.

crook•ed Not straight; bent or curving. We followed the <u>crooked</u> street to the end.

cud•dle To lie close and snug; nestle; snuggle. The kitten likes to <u>cuddle</u> up to its mother.

D

dar•ing Challenging someone to do something; challenging. Flying the small plane through the storm was a <u>daring</u> act.

dawn The first light that appears in the morning; daybreak. Greg woke up at <u>dawn</u> to get ready for his big trip.

deep•ly Intensely; extremely; in a great degree. Jenny thought <u>deeply</u> before she answered the teacher.

din•ing As in **dining room:** A room in which meals are served and eaten, as in a home or hotel. We eat breakfast and dinner in the <u>dining</u> room.

din·o·saur One of a large group of extinct reptiles that lived millions of years ago. No dinosaur lives on the earth today.

dir·i·gi·ble A large balloon that is shaped like a cigar, that is driven by a motor, and that can be steered. The dirigible moved slowly through the air, low in the sky.

dolls Toys that look like babies, children, or grown persons. My little sister likes to play with dolls.

done Completed; finished. The work is done.

don·key An animal that looks very much like a small horse. The children will have a ride on the donkey.

drag·on·ish Of the nature or character of a dragon; like a dragon. Except for being quite small, the bug looked very dragonish.

E

earth The planet on which people live. The earth is a very large place with many people.

edge A place where something ends; side. The glass of milk fell off the edge of the table.

ei·ther Any more so; also. Henry doesn't like tomatoes and he doesn't like apples either.

e·lec·ted Chosen by voting. The class elected Tony to be in charge of the book sale.

em•bar•rassed Caused to feel uncomfortable or ashamed. Robin was <u>embarrassed</u> about forgetting the birthday gift.

en•ter To enroll; to become a member or part of; join; to go or come into. Did Sarah <u>enter</u> her frog in the frog-jumping contest?

en•tire Having all the parts or elements; total; complete. The <u>entire</u> house was filled with boxes.

en•vy A feeling of jealousy and not being happy about someone else's good luck; to feel envy toward or because of. Tim said to Tina, "I <u>envy</u> you your new boat."

es•caped Got away; got free. The rabbit <u>escaped</u> from Betty and ran back into the woods.

eve•ry•bod•y Every person. <u>Everybody</u> on the team was out for the game.

ex•cept With the exception of; excluding; but. The store is open every day <u>except</u> one.

ex•er•cise Activity that trains or improves the body or the mind. Darlene will practice the new <u>exercise</u> every day to make her ankles strong.

ex•tra Additional; more than what is usual or needed. Papa made some <u>extra</u> bread in case more people came to the party.

F

fair Not in favor of any one more than another or others; just; according to the rules; a public showing of products or objects. It didn't seem <u>fair</u> to Theo that only he had to stay home.

fa·mil·iar Often heard or seen; knowing something well; friendly or close. As Jeff walked to school, he looked at the <u>familiar</u> houses and streets.

fault Something that is wrong with and spoils something else; the responsibility for a mistake. The accident was not the <u>fault</u> of anyone.

fa·vor·ite Liked best; a person or thing that is liked best. Do you have a <u>favorite</u> color?

fel·low A man or boy. Who is that dear little <u>fellow</u> with Mrs. Bloom?

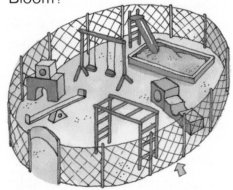

fence A structure that is used to surround, protect, or mark off an area. There is a high <u>fence</u> all around the playground.

fes·ti·vals Celebrations; holidays. One of my home town <u>festivals</u> is the May Apple Blossom celebration.

fig·ure A form or outline; shape. You will see what I mean if you look at the <u>figure</u> in the book.

fi·nal·ly At the end; at last. After several hours, the rain <u>finally</u> stopped.

fire The flame, heat, and light given off in burning; something burning. Cats like to lie by the <u>fire</u> and sleep.

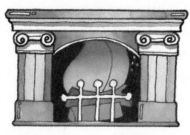

fire·place An opening in a room with a chimney leading up from it. It makes us feel snug and warm to have a fire in the <u>fireplace</u>.

foot The end part of the leg that people and other animals walk on or stand on. Pam tried on the new shoes, but the right one was too small for her <u>foot</u>.

308

for•est Many trees and plants covering a large area of ground; woods. We followed the path through the forest to the lake.

form To give form to; to make or produce; to fashion. We decided to form a baseball team in our neighborhood.

forth Forward. From that day forth, the man never went back to the city.

for•ward Toward what is in front or ahead. I am really looking forward to our summer trip.

fought Took part in battle with. The cat scratched and clawed as it fought against the dog.

foun•tain pen A pen that has a small tube inside that feeds ink to the writing point. Dad stopped to buy black ink for his fountain pen.

free•dom The condition of being free; able to move or act without being held back. Zebras live in freedom, playing and running freely.

fright•ened Made suddenly alarmed or afraid; terrified or scared. The animals were frightened by the forest fire.

fumb•ling Looking for in a clumsy way; handling clumsily or dropping. Mother was fumbling around in the box for the needles.

fun•ny Causing laughter; strange; odd. Jill heard a funny noise in the middle of the night.

fur•ry Like fur or covered with fur. Mimi was warm and snug under the furry blanket.

G

gal•loped Hurried or very fast movement of a four-footed animal. The race horses galloped to the finish line.

gift Something given; present; donation. Mona's birthday gift to Paco was a book.

gig•gling Laughing in a high, silly way. The girls were giggling as they watched the funny show.

glanced Took a quick look. Gram glanced out the window of the airplane at the passing clouds.

glared Gave an angry look; a strong unpleasant light. Tony glared at Robin when he tripped over her toy.

glo•ri•ous Full of glory; grand; magnificent. The earth was a glorious sight from the airship high in the sky.

grown-ups People who have come to full-growth; adults. The children and the grown-ups sat at different tables.

guar•ded Kept safe from harm or danger; protected; watched over or controlled. The dog guarded the house while the family was away.

gulp To swallow quickly, greedily, or in large amounts; to draw in or swallow air; gasp. Mother asked the children not to gulp their food.

H

ha•bit An action done so often or for so long that it is done without thinking. It was Mona's habit to put her books on the table when she came home from school.

half One of two equal parts of something. Mother gave half the blueberries to Mrs. Long and kept half for us.

hand•ker•chief A square, soft piece of cloth used to wipe the nose or face. Dad waved his handkerchief at the people on the bus.

han•dle The part of an object that is made to be grasped by the hands. If the door is closed, you must turn the handle to open it.

han•ky A short word for **handkerchief**, a soft piece of cloth, usually square, used especially to wipe the nose or face. When the little girl began to cry, her mother gave her a hanky.

hay•loft Loft in a barn or stable for storing hay. The children loved to play and read in the hayloft when they went to the country.

heart The part of the body that pumps blood. In his heart, Ted knew that he had been wrong to act as he did.

held Took and kept in the hands or arms; grasped, gripped. Amanda held the little kitten in her arms.

hind At the back; rear. Ted taught his dog to stand on its hind legs.

ho•la Spanish for "hello." Carlos called, "Hola!" when he saw Maria.

hook A bent piece of metal, wood, or other strong material that is used to hold or fasten something; to hang, fasten, or attach with a hook. Please put your coat on the hook.

hope•ful•ly In a manner having or showing hope. Meg waited hopefully for an answer to her letter.

hor•ri•ble Causing great fear or shock; very bad, ugly, or unpleasant. The horrible creaking sound scared the children.

horse A large four-legged animal with hooves, a long mane, and tail. Did you see the mare play with her baby horse?

311

hun•gry Wanting or needing food. The children were <u>hungry</u> after playing all afternoon.

hunt To look hard; to try to find something. Animals in the forest must <u>hunt</u> for food.

hus•tle To move or do something quickly. ''We will have to <u>hustle</u> if we want to catch the bus,'' said Jenny.

I

i•mag•i•na•tion The ability or power to create or form new images or ideas; the forming of pictures in the mind of things that are not really there. In her <u>imagination</u>, Mary was a princess in a kingdom of long ago.

in•ter•rupt•ed Broke in upon or stopped a person or persons while acting or speaking. Mrs. Long <u>interrupted</u> the party by saying that it was time to go.

J

jack•al An animal that looks somewhat like a dog. A <u>jackal</u> often eats the food that other animals leave.

Ja•pan An island country in the Pacific Ocean. My grandparents visited the city of Tokyo while they were in <u>Japan</u>.

judg•ing Deciding the winner in a contest; deciding on questions in a court of law. Everybody wanted to watch the <u>judging</u> of the homemade pie contest.

Ju•pi•ter The largest planet; fifth closest planet to the sun. <u>Jupiter</u> has twelve known moons.

312

K

kept Continued to have, hold, or do. The ball <u>kept</u> rolling until it reached the <u>street</u>.

kitch•en A room where food is cooked. Good smells come from the <u>kitchen</u> when Mother makes dinner.

L

liz•ard An animal that has a long, scaly body, four legs, and a long tail. A <u>lizard</u> is an animal that lives in warm places, such as the desert.

lone•ly Unhappy from being alone; away from others; alone. The <u>lonely</u> house was in the woods far from the town.

M

ma•chine A device that does some particular job. Tom and Rico had a plan for making a flying <u>machine</u>.

ma•má Spanish for "mama." <u>Mamá</u> will begin her trip today.

Mars The seventh largest planet; fourth closest planet to the sun. The Viking spacecrafts have landed on <u>Mars</u>.

mas•ter A person who has power or control over something. The man said, "I can train any dog to mind its <u>master</u>."

may•or The person who is the official head of a city or town government. The <u>mayor</u> spoke to a large crowd of people about the plan for new city lights.

meant Had in mind; wanted to do or say. Paco <u>meant</u> to send the letter to Juan instead of Carmela.

313

med•al A flat piece of metal that is often shaped like a coin. Jason got a <u>medal</u> for the best story in the story contest.

Mer•cu•ry The closest planet to the sun. <u>Mercury</u> is the fastest moving planet.

mid•dle Halfway between two things, sides, or times. Our swing is in the <u>middle</u> of the backyard.

min•ute A unit of time equal to sixty seconds; a moment in time; instant. "I will be able to help you in a <u>minute</u>," said the teacher.

mon•key A furry animal that has long arms and legs, and hands and feet that are used for grasping and climbing. The <u>monkey</u> danced and chattered in his jungle home.

mon•sters Imaginary creatures that are huge and frightening. Jeff and Jenny will dress up as <u>monsters</u> for the school play.

mo•tion•less Not moving. Mike stands <u>motionless</u> as the snake moves slowly away.

moun•tain A mass of land that rises very high above the land around it. The top of the <u>mountain</u> was covered with snow even in summer.

mouse•traps Traps for catching mice. We set four <u>mousetraps</u>, but we didn't catch a single mouse.

mouth•ful An amount of food that is or can be held in the mouth at one time. Ted slowly chewed the large <u>mouthful</u> of food.

mu•si•cian A person who is skilled in playing a musical instrument, composing music, or singing. Louise wants to be a <u>musician</u> when she grows up.

mys•te•ri•ous•ly In a way very hard or impossible to explain or understand; puzzlingly. <u>Mysteriously</u>, the paper began to fly around the room.

N

nar•row Not wide or broad. The path was so <u>narrow</u> that the children had to walk one behind the other.

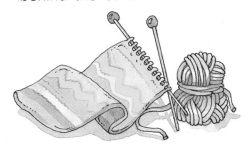

nee•dles Thin rods that are used in knitting. Mother showed Jane how to hold the knitting <u>needles</u>.

Nep•tune Fourth largest planet and eighth closest to the sun. <u>Neptune</u> appears green when seen through a telescope.

ner•vous•ly In a tense or upset manner. The man walked <u>nervously</u> until the train arrived.

New York Cit•y The largest city in the United States, located in New York State. Our family will take a trip to <u>New York City</u> and visit many places of interest.

nonsense A way of talking or acting that is silly and makes no sense. Father said, "It's time to stop playing and go to bed. No <u>nonsense</u>, now."

O

O•lym•pic Games Modern international athletic contests modeled on the games of ancient Greece, held every four years in a different country. The last <u>Olympic Games</u> were in the United States.

o•pos•sum A small, furry animal that lives in trees. If an opossum is scared, it will lie very still instead of running away.

or•ange A round fruit that has a thick orange or yellow skin and a sweetish juice. Pam ate an orange and two apples.

or•bit The path that a planet or other heavenly body follows as it moves in a circle around another heavenly body; to move in an orbit around a heavenly body. The moon makes an orbit around the earth about once a month.

or•di•nar•y Commonly used; regular; usual; not different in any way from others. Today started out as an ordinary day, but it turned into a day I'll never forget.

P

pair A set of things meant to be used together; a single thing made up of two parts. A person has a pair of eyes, ears, hands, and feet.

pan•try A small room for storing food, dishes, and silver. The shelves of the pantry were filled with cans of food.

pa•pá Spanish for "papa." Papá and Ramon took a walk through the park.

par•don A refusal to blame or punish; forgiveness. When Willy stepped on the woman's foot, he said, "I beg your pardon!"

par•tridge A bird that is hunted as game. A partridge has a fat body and feathers of different colors.

par•ty A gathering of people to have a good time. Ted asked all his friends to his birthday party.

pas•sen•ger A person who travels in an automobile, bus, train, airplane, or boat. Jo was the only passenger on the bus who was going to Newport.

peace Freedom from fighting; quiet or calm. The message on the card was "Peace on earth."

peb•ble A small stone that is usually round and smooth. Sue thought the pebble she found was gold.

per•son A man, woman, or child; human being; individual. The person who won the contest was my friend Anne.

pi•lot A person who operates an aircraft or spacecraft. The pilot announced that the flight would take two hours.

pit•y A cause for regret, or a feeling of sorrow and sympathy for the unhappiness of another. What a pity it is that Jane won't be at the party!

pla•net One of the nine large bodies that move around the sun. Earth is a planet; it circles the sun.

plas•ter A mixture of lime, sand, and water that becomes hard, smooth material when dry. When the plaster was almost dry, the children pressed their hands into it to show their form.

pleas•ure A feeling of delight and happiness; something that gives a feeling of joy and happiness. It was always a pleasure to visit Grandmother.

plen•ty A large amount; as much as is needed. Tony has <u>plenty</u> of room in his new coat.

Plu•to The furthest planet from the sun. The temperature of <u>Pluto</u> is about −300°F (−184°C).

po•ems Forms of writing in verse that express imaginative thought or strong feeling. The children made up <u>poems</u> for Mandy's birthday and read them at the party.

po•lite•ly In a way showing good manners or a consideration for others; courteously. The woman smiled <u>politely</u> and said, "Thank you," to the man who had given her directions.

pos•si•bly By any possibility. We looked as hard as we <u>possibly</u> could to find the box.

prac•tice To do something over and over to gain skill; the doing of something over and over again to gain skill. Emily decided to <u>practice</u> her cartwheels to get better at them.

pre•cious Having great value. The toy train was old and ordinary, but it was <u>precious</u> to Scott.

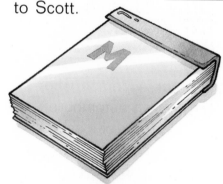

print•ed Wrote in letters like those made by type, instead of script. Meg <u>printed</u> her name on the library card.

pri•vate Belonging to a particular person or group; not meant to be shared with others; not public. Meg wrote her secret ideas in a <u>private</u> book.

prob•a•bly Almost surely; most likely. We will <u>probably</u> have chicken for dinner.

prom•ise Words given by a person, saying that something will or will not be done or happen. Jason kept his <u>promise</u> that he would take the message to his grandmother in person.

pro•pel•ler A device made up of blades mounted at an angle around a hub. When the <u>propeller</u> of a plane turns, it moves the air and the plane goes forward.

pur•ple The color that is made by mixing red and blue; having the color purple. Gold and <u>purple</u> are the colors of our school.

Q

quiv•er•ing Shaking slightly; shivering. The dog was <u>quivering</u> because he was frightened by the loud noise.

R

rath•er More readily or willingly. Lucy would <u>rather</u> have a dog than a cat for a pet.

ra•ven A bird that looks very much like a crow but is larger. A <u>raven</u> has black feathers and a sharp cry.

reared Went up on the back legs. The horse <u>reared</u> when it came to the fence.

re•gards Best wishes. Mother asked Mr. Bloom to give her <u>regards</u> to his family.

riv•er A large stream of water that flows naturally and empties into a lake, ocean, or other river. Don and Billy will sail their boat down the <u>river</u> to the sea.

roar To make a loud, deep sound or cry. All the animals in the forest heard the lion <u>roar</u>.

rob·ber A person who robs, or steals. The <u>robber</u> took a necklace and some money.

ro·bot A machine that looks somewhat like a person and that can do some of the same things that a person can. The toy <u>robot</u> could talk, move, and pick up things.

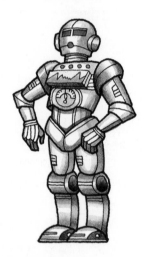

roll·er skate A skate having small wheels on the bottom, used for skating on a flat surface. Where is my left <u>roller skate</u>?

roll·ing Moving by turning over and over; moving in a smooth manner. Mother was <u>rolling</u> up the rug so that she could clean the floor.

roost·er A male chicken. We can hear the <u>rooster</u> crowing early in the morning.

S

salt A white substance found in sea water and in the ground, used to season and preserve food. Too much <u>salt</u> is not good for you.

sand·bags Bags filled with or designed to hold sand, used for such purposes as adding weight or controlling floods. The balloon rose as the <u>sandbags</u> were thrown over the side of the basket.

sat·el·lites Heavenly bodies that move around other bodies larger than they are. <u>Satellites</u> in space tell us about the weather and speed telephone calls.

Sat•urn The second largest planet and sixth closest to the sun. *Voyager I* took pictures of the rings of <u>Saturn</u>.

sau•cers Small shallow dishes, especially those for holding cups. Mother told Emily to put <u>saucers</u> under the cups.

scare•dy cats Words used to tease or urge people to do something they are afraid to do. The girls were <u>scaredy cats</u> because they would not dive from the high board.

sci•en•tists People who know a great deal about some branch of science. <u>Scientists</u> have learned a lot about space.

scoot•er A vehicle having a narrow footboard mounted on two wheels and a handle for steering. If you put one foot on the scooter and push with the other against the ground, the <u>scooter</u> will move forward.

sculp•tor A person who produces a sculpture. A <u>sculptor</u> makes works of art from clay or plaster.

sculp•ture The art of carving or making figures or designs; the figure or design that is made this way. Ned admired the <u>sculpture</u> of a bird.

searched Looked carefully in order to find something. John <u>searched</u> through the house for his mitten—then he found that the dog had it!

se•ri•ous Having a solemn, thoughtful manner; grave. Tom had a <u>serious</u> look on his face when he told his mother about the accident.

shall A form of the verb **to be** used in the future tense with the words **I** and **we.** I <u>shall</u> be late for dinner tonight.

share To use with another or others; to divide into portions and give to others as well as to oneself. Sue and Gloria <u>share</u> a room at home.

shiv•ered Shook; trembled. Linda <u>shivered</u> because she was wet and cold.

shov•eled Dug and moved with a shovel. Ed and Karen shoveled the snow from the porch and the sidewalk.

shrugged Raised or drew up the shoulders to show doubt or lack of interest. Robert shrugged when his mother asked if he wanted something to eat.

shut•tle A vehicle that makes trips back and forth between two places. A shuttle can be a spaceship, a train, a car, a bus, a plane, or a truck.

si•lent Completely quiet; still. The house was dark and silent in the middle of the night.

sil•ver A shiny white metal that is soft and easily shaped; the color of silver; made or coated with silver. Mother was knitting with silver needles.

sin•gle Only one. Peter counted every single penny, nickel, dime, and quarter in the box.

skate•board A low, flat board that has wheels on the bottom, used for riding. Bob and Mark made their own skateboard from a board and some wheels.

skunk A black animal that has a bushy tail and white stripes along its back. Can you tell me what a skunk smells like?

smooth Even, easy or gentle in movement; having a surface that is not rough. Our new car gives us such a smooth ride.

snick•ered Laughed in a sly, disrespectful way. Nan was sorry she had snickered at her baby brother and made him cry.

soar To fly high in the air. We watched the plane soar over the mountain.

322

soft•ly Gently or lightly; not harshly or sharply. John spoke softly to the baby so that she wouldn't be scared and cry.

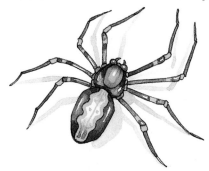

spi•der A small animal with four pairs of legs, a body that is divided into two parts, and no wings. Have you ever watched a spider spin a web to catch a fly?

splen•did Beautiful or magnificent; very good; excellent. The children did a splendid job of putting on the play.

spoons Utensils with a small, shallow bowl at one end of a handle. We use spoons to eat soup and breakfast cereal.

squeak To make a short, thin, high sound or cry. All the doors squeak when you open or close them.

steered Guided the course of. Father carefully steered the car along the road up the hill.

stom•ach The part of the body that receives and begins to digest food that has been swallowed. Tim said, "I ate so much that my stomach hurts!"

stored Put away for future use. The squirrel stored nuts for the winter.

storm A strong wind with heavy rain, hail, sleet, or snow. Everyone ran inside when they saw the storm coming.

stow•a•way A person who conceals himself or herself on a ship or airplane, especially in order to get free passage. After the plane had left the airport, the pilot discovered a stowaway among the passengers.

straight Not bent, curved, or crooked. The teacher asked the children to stand in a straight line.

strange Odd or unusual; not familiar. Jeff saw a strange car in front of his house when he came home.

stream A body of flowing water, smaller than a river. The children took off their shoes and walked in the <u>stream</u>.

stripe A long narrow band. These socks have a yellow <u>stripe</u> around the edge.

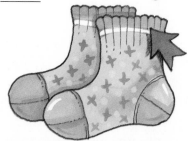

strokes Marks made by a pen, pencil, brush, or other thing. The little child made <u>strokes</u> that looked a bit like letters.

strug•gled Made a great effort. The boys <u>struggled</u> to get the boat in the water.

stub•born Not giving in; not yielding. Mike is <u>stubborn</u>. He will keep trying for a basket until he gets one.

stump The lower part of a tree trunk. When a tree is cut down, only the <u>stump</u> is left.

sug•ar A white or brown sweet substance. Mother needed <u>sugar</u> to make the cookies.

sure•ly Without doubt; truly; positively. <u>Surely</u> you will not forget Luz's birthday.

sus•pi•cious Causing suspicion; feeling or showing suspicion. Mother is always <u>suspicious</u> of strangers.

swal•low To cause food to pass from the mouth to the stomach. Beth had to <u>swallow</u> her food before she could answer her mother.

sweat•er A warm knitted piece of clothing worn over the upper part of the body. Mona knitted herself a beautiful blue <u>sweater</u>.

swing To move or turn in a curved motion. A monkey can <u>swing</u> from tree to tree through the forest.

T

Tai•wan An island country in Asia. Taiwan is not a very big island.

taught Helped a person to learn; showed how. Father taught Tim how to play basketball.

tear•ing Pulling or becoming pulled apart. Clara opened the package quickly, tearing the box and paper.

tears Drops of clear, salty liquid that come from the eye. Tears came to Jane's eyes when she cut her foot.

ter•ri•ble Causing fear or terror; awful. Everyone stopped talking when they heard the terrible noise of the crash.

tests Methods to find out the quality of something. After many tests were done, the boat was put in the water.

they're Contraction for **they are.** Sue and Ned are away on a trip. They're in Mexico.

thread A very thin cord that is used in sewing and weaving cloth. Mother used a piece of thread to fix the tear in her coat.

threw Past tense of **throw.** Louie threw the ball straight into the basket.

throb•bing Beating or pounding heavily and fast. Mona's heart was throbbing after she had run all the way from school to her house.

throw To send up into or through the air. "Throw the ball to first base!" yelled Coach Red.

thrown In the phrase **thrown away:** rejected, discarded. The old newspapers were put in a box to be thrown away.

tí•a Spanish for "aunt." My mother's sister is my Tía Lupita.

ti•ny Very small. The baby turtle was tiny when it was born.

tí•o Spanish for "uncle." My mother's brother is my Tío Paco.

tog·gles Pins, bolts, or rods put through the eye of a rope or the link of a chain to prevent slipping, to tighten, or to secure an attachment. The aeronaut checked the ropes, sandbags, and <u>toggles</u>.

to·ma·toes Round, juicy fruits, usually red, that grow on vines. We will grow <u>tomatoes</u> in the garden this year.

town An area in which people live and work. Our <u>town</u> is a small <u>town</u> on a lake.

tre·men·dous Very large or great; enormous. A <u>tremendous</u> number of people were at the show.

trou·ble A difficult or dangerous situation. Father had <u>trouble</u> with the car as he drove over the high mountain.

truth Something that is true; the quality of being true, honest, or sincere. It is always better to tell the <u>truth</u> than to lie.

twisted Changed from the usual shape of something. The metal had been <u>twisted</u> into a new shape.

U

um·brel·la A circular piece of cloth or plastic stretched on a framework that can be folded up when it is not needed. Mother said, "It looks as if it might rain. Take your <u>umbrella</u> when you go out."

un·buck·ling Undoing or unfastening a buckle or buckles. Carmela began <u>unbuckling</u> her seat belt as soon as the plane came to a stop.

U·nit·ed States A country mainly in North America, made up of fifty states. We all live in the <u>United States</u>; it is our country.

up·draft An upward movement of air. The balloon was carried away on the <u>updraft</u>.

U·ra·nus The third largest planet and seventh closest to the sun. Uranus has five known moons.

V

valve A device that controls the flow of liquids or gases. Jacob put air into the ball through a valve.

vent A hole or other opening through which gas or liquid passes. The hot air passed out of the room through a vent.

Ve·nus The sixth largest planet and second closest to the sun. On a clear night, Venus can be seen from Earth without a telescope.

W

warn·ing Putting on guard by giving notice beforehand; giving advice or notice to. The yellow blinking traffic light was a warning to the drivers.

weath·er The condition of the air or atmosphere at a particular time and place. The weather has been cold and rainy for several days.

weight A burden or load; the amount of heaviness of a person or thing. The weight of too many people made the boat sink.

whis·tle To make a clear, sharp sound by forcing air out through closed lips or through the teeth; a whistling sound. My dog will come if I whistle for him.

wires Thin rods of metal. The telephone wires go from inside our house to the pole outside.

wob·ble To move from side to side in an unsteady or shaky way. Father can fix the leg of the table so it won't <u>wobble</u> anymore.

won·drous Wonderful. The old castle was the most <u>wondrous</u> place the children had ever seen.

wool·ly Made of or like wool; covered with wool or some similar material. Our dog is so <u>woolly</u> that it is hard to see his eyes and nose.

world The earth. If you could visit any place in the <u>world</u>, what place would you pick?

World's Fair A very large show with exhibits about science, business, and industry; also has amusements, food, and cultural activities. Chicago held a <u>World's Fair</u> in the late 1800's.

Y

yes·ter·day The day before today. <u>Yesterday</u> we started painting the house. Today we will paint some more.

yo-yo A toy consisting of two disks connected at their center by a pin around which a string is wound. Can you make a <u>yo-yo</u> go up and down?

you'd Contraction for **you would** or **you had.** Tony said, "I don't know the answers. <u>You'd</u> better ask someone else."

you'll Contraction for **you will** or **you shall.** If <u>you'll</u> read the directions and <u>follow</u> them, <u>you'll</u> have a kite that will fly.

young Having lived or existed for a short time; not old. When my father was <u>young</u>, he liked to play basketball.

This part of *Friends Aloft* is a review of letters and the sounds they stand for. Looking carefully at these letters will help you know how to say and read many new words.

Lessons

1 Initial Consonants

Letters stand for sounds at the beginning of words.

___ix ___isters ___ang ___illy ___ongs.

The sentence above does not make sense. The words do not have the letter that makes the beginning sound. What letter could you use to finish the sentence?

Number your paper from 1 to 5. Write the sentences below. Fill in the missing letters. Choose the letters from those in the box. Be sure the words make sense in the sentence. Begin each sentence with a capital letter.

m	w	g	p	s

1. I ___aw a ___urprise for me ___itting on the table.
2. I ___ulled the ___aper off the ___ackage and ___eeked inside.
3. ___uess what I ___ot!
4. ___y ___other had ___ade ___ittens for ___e.
5. They ___ere ___arm and ___oolly.

330

2 Initial Consonants

Some beginning sounds can be spelled more than one way.

Read the words below. Look at the underlined letters.

<u>f</u>ather	<u>h</u>ole	<u>n</u>ew	<u>r</u>ight
<u>ph</u>otograph	<u>wh</u>ole	<u>kn</u>ew	<u>wr</u>ite

What two letters can spell the sound you hear at the beginning of *father*?

What sound can the letters *wh* stand for?

What two letters can spell the sound you hear at the beginning of *new*?

What two letters can spell the sound you hear at the beginning of *right*?

Number your paper from 1 to 8. Read each group of words. Write the two words from each group that begin with the same sound.

1.	knock	2.	with	3.	rocket	4.	pony
	king		who		wrapped		forth
	noise		half		work		phone

5.	wrong	6.	kite	7.	who's	8.	wished
	word		known		woods		wrote
	river		nobody		hook		rose

word work

3 Final Consonants

Letters stand for sounds at the end of words. Some ending sounds can be spelled more than one way.

Read the words below. Look at the underlined letters.

cactu<u>s</u>   mai<u>l</u>   abou<u>t</u>   squea<u>k</u>   stea<u>m</u>

gra<u>ss</u>   do<u>ll</u>   cra<u>ck</u>

Two *s*'s can make the same sound as one *s*. What other letter can you say this about?

What two letters can spell the sound you hear at the end of *look*?

Number your paper from 1 to 6. Write the sentences. Fill in the missing letters. Use letters from the box.

s	ss	l	ll	t	k	ck	m

1. My dad too__ u__ to the circu__.
2. My favorite anima__ was a funny sea__.
3. It had a specia__ poo__ with gla__ sides.
4. It could dive to the botto__ and swi__ ba__ up.
5. It would snea__ up behind the trainer and pu__ something out of her pocke__.
6. Tha__ was a good tri__ ! Can you gue__ wha__ trea__ was hidden there?

332

4 Short Vowels and Graphemic Bases

Read each word in the box below. Look at the underlined letter that spells each short vowel sound.

a	**e**	**i**	**o**	**u**
s<u>a</u>d	b<u>e</u>d	tr<u>i</u>ck	n<u>o</u>t	<u>u</u>p

A. Number your paper from 1 to 5. Read each sentence. Think of one vowel that will fit *all* of the blanks in the sentence. Then write the sentence on your paper.

1. I knew a m___n who h___d a c___t.
2. He watched it r___n and j___mp.
3. Th___n he f___d his p___t.
4. It would s___t beside h___m and l___ck ___ts fur.
5. Then it would h___p into a b___x and take a nap.

B. Number your paper from 1 to 5. Write the words below. Next to each word, write a word from the box that rhymes.

1. rag   2. ten   3. rock   4. trip   5. luck

when	ship	click	truck	drum
mad	clock	that	brag	fox

5 Initial Consonant Clusters

The sounds of some letters blend together. Read the words below. Listen for the sounds of the underlined letters.

<u>c</u>lean   <u>g</u>lue   <u>fl</u>at   <u>fr</u>ont   <u>cr</u>y   <u>dr</u>op

A. Number your paper from 1 to 6. Say the picture names. Use the letters underlined above to make the words. Write the words on your paper.

1. ___ag   2. ___ow   3. ___ess

4. ___asses   5. ___oud   6. ___og

B. Write the following story on your paper. Fill in the letters for the beginning sounds. Choose letters from those in the box.

| cl | gl | fl | fr | cr | dr |

I saw a strange ___eature. It was ___ying in the sky. It came ___oser to me. Its eyes ___owed brightly, and ___ames came out of its mouth. I felt ___ightened. It was a ___agon! Then I woke up. I was ___ad it was only a ___eam.

6 Initial Consonant Clusters

The letter *s* often blends with another letter at the beginning of a word. Read each word below. Listen for the sounds of the underlined letters.

<u>sc</u>ooter   <u>sk</u>in   <u>sm</u>ashed   <u>sn</u>ug   <u>st</u>ubborn

Number your paper from 1 to 10. Read each riddle. Use letters underlined above to make a word that answers each riddle. Write the words on your paper.

1. Not big   ___all

2. Frightened   ___ared

3. Cold and white   ___ow

4. Begin   ___art

5. Something warm around your neck   ___arf

6. A little animal with a big smell   ___unk

7. A place where you buy things   ___ore

8. Something good to eat   ___ack

9. What you do when you are happy   ___ile

10. Wheels for your feet   ___ates

335

7 Final Consonant Clusters

Sometimes two letters blend together at the end of a word. Say each word below. Listen for the sounds of the underlined letters.

le<u>ft</u>   almo<u>st</u>   dri<u>nk</u>

Write each poem below on your paper. Fill in the missing letters. Choose letters from those in the box.

ft	st	nk

1. The pet I like mo___ is my turtle,
    Yet when it comes to going fa___,
    My be___ pet always comes in la___!

2. There's a rope swing in the barn.
    It gives me a swi___ li___
    Into the so___ haylo___.

3. In my room I have a tru___.
    It's a wonderful place to keep old ju___.
    When I have to clean things up,
    I drop everything in—kupli___, kuplu___!

4. What color is the kitchen si___?
    It's pi___,
    I thi___.

8 Long Vowels and Graphemic Bases

The words below show two ways to spell the long *a* vowel sound. Read the words. Look at the underlined letters.

sh<u>a</u>k<u>e</u>   st<u>ay</u>

Now read the two words below. Look at the underlined letters. They show two ways to spell the long *i* vowel sound.

s<u>i</u>d<u>e</u>   l<u>igh</u>t

Number your paper from 1 to 12. Read each set of words. Write the word that has a long *a* or long *i* vowel sound.

1.	kick	2.	came	3.	bring	4.	splash
	kids		caught		bright		skate
	kite		catch		brand		swift

5.	fine	6.	pitch	7.	price	8.	animal
	figure		plant		print		aside
	first		plane		part		any

9.	gray	10.	sharp	11.	bake	12.	straws
	grin		shades		basket		string
	grab		ship		barn		stripe

337

9 Long Vowels and Graphemic Bases

Read the two words below. Look at the underlined letters. The long o vowel sound can be spelled in these two ways.

<u>stro</u>ke c<u>oa</u>ch

Now read the word below. The underlined letters spell the long u vowel sound.

<u>u</u>s<u>e</u>

Number your paper from 1 to 10. Read each sentence and the words that follow it. Write the sentence using the word that has a long o or a long u vowel sound.

1. There once was a _____ giant.   good   huge
2. He was usually _____.   alone   hungry
3. One day he _____ up feeling sad.   got   woke
4. "I have no friends," he _____.   sobbed   moaned
5. Then he saw a _____.   toad   frog
6. He _____ to it.   talked   spoke
7. "I _____ you will play with me."   hope   think
8. "Please don't _____."   return   refuse
9. The two laughed and _____.   jumped   joked
10. They played together that _____ day.   summer   whole

10 Long Vowels and Graphemic Bases

Read the words below. Look at the underlined letters.
The long e vowel sound is spelled in two ways.

f<u>ee</u>d   sh<u>e</u>

Number your paper from 1 to 12. Read each
sentence below. Find the word with the long e vowel
sound. Write the long e words on your paper.
Underline the letter or letters that stand for this sound.

1. My cousin Jo helped me make a car.
2. We used an old crate.
3. I found some good wheels.
4. Jo painted everything green.
5. Then Jo and I went to a quiet street.
6. It had a steep hill.
7. I sat on the car, then pulled up my feet.
8. I soon was zooming at quite a speed!
9. I dug my heels into the ground.
10. I could feel them scrape the sidewalk.
11. This kind of car may be bad for my shoes.
12. I think it needs brakes!

11 Initial Consonant Digraphs

Two or three letters may stand for one sound. Say the words below. Look at the underlined letters. Listen for the one sound the two letters make.

<u>sh</u>ip   <u>th</u>ank   <u>wh</u>istle   <u>ch</u>ild

Number your paper from 1 to 12. Use the underlined letters above to make a word for each sentence. Write the word on your paper. Be sure it makes sense in the sentence.

1. I had a surprise ___en I woke up.
2. The world had ___anged in the night.
3. Everything was covered with ___ite.
4. The yard was covered with a ___ick blanket of snow.
5. ___at a wonderful surprise!
6. I ran outside without ___inking to put on warm clothes.
7. My teeth ___attered.
8. I ___ivered.
9. I ___ook.
10. My ___eeks turned red.
11. I ran into the house to put on warm ___ings.
12. Then Mom and I ___oveled the sidewalk together.

12 Final Consonant Digraphs

Read the following words. Listen for how the two or three underlined letters make one sound.

teach splash bring crutch

What are two ways of spelling the sound you hear at the end of the word *coach*?

Read the story below. Look at the end of each underlined word.

This morning everything seemed to go wrong. I had no time to finish breakfast. I had to rush to catch the bus. On the way I tripped. I got a bad scratch on my leg. I did reach the bus in time, but I had not remembered my lunch. It's no fun to sit and watch everyone else munch! I wish I could start today over again.

Number your paper from 1 to 4. Write each word below. Next to each word, write the words from the story that end with the same sound and letters.

1. ostrich **2.** patch **3.** foolish **4.** song

13 Diphthongs

Read the words below. What letters spell the same sound in the first pair? What letters spell the same sound in the second pair?

acc<u>ou</u>nt all<u>ow</u>ed   p<u>oi</u>son b<u>oy</u>s

A. Number your paper from 1 to 6. Use the letters to make a word for each sentence. Write the words.

1. The ___l is an interesting bird.   ow oy

2. It makes a strange s___nd.   oi ou

3. Have you heard a n___se in the
   night that goes "Who, who?"   oi ow

4. You may have heard its v___ce.   ou oi

5. One lives in the woods near our h___se. oy ou

6. I enj___ hearing it.   oy ow

B. Read the first word in each row. Listen for the sound of the underlined letters. Write another word from the row that has the same sound.

1. ar<u>ou</u>nd   spoil   frown   destroy

2. t<u>oy</u>s   noisy   bounce   flower

3. gr<u>ow</u>led   joy   voices   mountain

4. c<u>oi</u>n   down   boy   pounds

14 *r*-Controlled Vowels

The letter *r* changes the sound of the vowel it follows.

Look at each word pair below. Are the vowel sounds the same in—

cat and car?

help and her?

tug and turn?

fish and first?

won and work?

A. Number your paper from 1 to 4. From each list write the two words that *rhyme*.

1.	**2.**	**3.**	**4.**
hurt	lonely	work	fun
hum	worry	want	fur
dirt	sunny	cent	her
dim	furry	clerk	hen

B. Number your paper from 1 to 4. From each list write the two words in which *r* changes the vowel sound.

1.	**2.**	**3.**	**4.**
perhaps	crate	rim	worth
price	cart	thirty	wrapped
press	sharp	broken	arms
park	shrugged	burned	rags

343

15 Syllable Generalizations

When you come to a new word in your reading, it may help to work on one small part at a time. Each word part is called a *syllable*.

Read these words. Each has one vowel sound. Each has one syllable.

> can   pet   kick   stop   duck

Now read these words.

> basket   cactus   floppy

Each of these words has two syllables. Say each word. How many vowel sounds do you hear?

> Every syllable must have a sounded vowel.

Number your paper from 1 to 15. Say each word below to yourself. How many vowel sounds do you hear? Write **1** if the word has one syllable. Write **2** if the word has two syllables.

1. silver
2. large
3. forest
4. monkey
5. scratch
6. grin
7. also
8. bounce
9. berry
10. church
11. orbit
12. brightly
13. dinner
14. strange
15. geese

344